A Guide to

CONVEYANCING RESIDENTIAL PROPERTY

The Easyway

Revised Edition

Alan Stewart

Editor: Roger Sproston

D1146819

Easyway Guides

© Straightforward Co Ltd 2020

ISBN
978-1-913342-03-6

Printed in Great Britain by 4 edge www.4edge.co.uk

Cover design by Straightforward Graphics

Contents

Introduction

Conclusion and summary of the conveyancing process

Glossary of terms

Appendix 1

Standard letters used in conveyancing

Appendix 2

Sample conveyancing costs when using a licensed conveyancer

Appendix 3. Sample forms used in conveyancing

Index

****

Introduction

This book, updated to **2020**, is not a substitute for a qualified professional and is not presented as such. The information contained within is for use as guidance and at all times the advice of professionals should be sought, as only the extremely confident and experienced lay person, or actual practitioner can buy or sell property alone. In addition, if a mortgage is involved, the lender will insist on a qualified conveyancer.

Risks of DIY Conveyancing

Mistakes made during conveyancing transactions can be relatively trivial, for example carrying out the wrong search and having to pay a search fee twice, or extremely serious, for example misinterpreting a search result and buying an un-saleable property or finding that following completion it is not possible to register the transaction. When acting in a sale, failure to understand your obligations and responsibilities can lead to giving information for which the buyer can later sue, or being conned by the buyer into parting with money or reducing the price.

So, as stated above, usually when buying or selling residential property, solicitors or licensed conveyancers are normally used in order to ensure that the transaction proceeds smoothly. Both are regulated professionals whose governing bodies require that they be insured and properly regulated. Licensed conveyancers are regulated by the Council of Licensed Conveyancers, solicitors by the Solicitors Regulation Authority or Law Society. Both carry out the process of buying and selling property in a similar way. There are several legal differences between the professions.

Conveyancers are allowed to represent both buyer and seller, whereas solicitors generally don't because of conflict of interest.

Similarly, licensed conveyancers need not tell their client if they have received a commission from a marketing or referral agency, whereas solicitors must disclose such commissions. In general, licensed conveyancers may be more suited to a lower value or uncomplicated sale-and it will be much cheaper. If the sale is complex and expensive then a solicitor will be better suited.

Another development in 2019 is that new rules for conveyancers are now in place in Britain aimed at helping home buyers make a more informed choice when buying a property.

All property lawyers must now publish price, service and quality information on their websites, or in alternative formats if requested, as part of a cross-industry push to empower consumers and foster innovation and competition across the legal services market.

The Council for Licensed Conveyancers (CLC) said that all property lawyers will now have to display certain information including costs and provide examples of their fees that cover a broad range of services and transaction types.

This might include information on conveyancing timescales and links to third party feedback platforms and a buyer should be able to easily identify who regulates the firm. For lawyers regulated by the CLC, this includes displaying the CLC secure badge in a prominent place.

All lawyers need to display details of their complaints process including access to the Legal Ombudsman and redress information and while lawyers do not need to disclose specific details of referral arrangements on their website, they must say if they enter into such agreements and the average fee, or range of fees, they pay.

However, notwithstanding the above. the actual processes of conveyancing are usually a mystery to both buyer and seller who are not privy to the procedures. The aim of this brief but concise book is to throw some light on the basic processes, thus ensuring that those who are involved at least have some understanding of what is happening and can question those acting for them at any given point. The book should be read in conjunction with "A Straightforward Guide to Buying and Selling Property" which deals with the more general aspects such as the involvement of estate agents.

Although it is safe to say that the average basic conveyance of a leasehold flat or freehold house is relatively simple and unproblematic, there are still fundamental ground rules which one must observe. When purchasing a leasehold flat for example, particularly in a multi-occupied block, the lease has to be very closely scrutinised and all the covenants in the lease understood. Leases can be unintelligible documents, couched in redundant language, badly laid out and misleading at the best of times.

Leases contain landlord and tenants covenants, which impose rights and obligations on the respective parties, particularly in relation to repairing obligations and service charge and ground rent payments. Other covenants may impose an onerous burden on the leaseholder and quite often only an experienced eye can pick this up. Likewise, the Freehold transfer document may contain obligations, which can only be picked up or understood, by an experienced eye.

Therefore, even if you decide to carry out conveyancing yourself you should always get a sound second opinion concerning the lease or freehold document.

What about online conveyancing?

Traditionally, homebuyers have used local solicitors or conveyancers, often recommended by their estate agent or mortgage lender. However, online conveyancing is a growing area that is transforming the industry – generally for the better.

Online conveyancing companies sell their services over the web, usually backed up by a call centre. They are often based in business parks and are effectively warehouses of fully trained conveyancers dealing with thousands of property transactions. They are usually much more efficient and better value as a result of economies of scale and not being based in city centres. Like ordinary solicitors, the quality of service can be mixed. You deal with them via email and telephone and never see them face to face. Some online conveyancers' business models means your file is on a system and you talk to different people each time.

This can be frustrating. Others allocate your file to one person which provides you with a point of contract.

Good online conveyancers should enable you to access your file 24/7, so you can see its progress. This is useful because when sellers badger buyers for updates you can tell them immediately. Be aware that many websites describe themselves as online conveyancing, but are actually just price comparison websites which will get quotes for you from third party conveyancers or solicitors. This can be very helpful in finding a cheap service, but you can't be sure about sort of quality of service you are going to get from whoever you end up with. However, conveyancers – whether online or not – cannot deal with complex legal issues, and you should then go with a solicitor.

As we will see later, there are two forms of conveyancing in existence, registered and unregistered. The former means that the ownership of land and all that entails, including extent of ownership, is registered at the Land Registry. The very fact of registration ensures that legal title can be verified. Unregistered land has to be proven through production of deeds, which can be time consuming and problematic. Land Registration has been compulsory in the United Kingdom for a while now, but it is still a fact that a fairly significant amount of all property is unregistered.

This book details the processes of conveyancing a it affects both registered and unregistered land. It then goes on to deal with the advanced stages of conveyancing as it affects unregistered land and also the process of conveyancing registered land. Following the conclusion, which combines a complete summary of the conveyancing process, is a glossary of terms and a list of useful address. There are appendices, containing sample letters and a summary of conveyancing costs plus a list of forms used in conveyancing residential property.

**

Chapter 1

Conveyancing In Context

Conveyancing, or the practice of conveyancing, is about how to transfer the ownership of land and property from one person or organisation to another. Land and property can include freehold property, leasehold property (residential) or can include business leases. It is principally the conveyance of residential property that this book is concerned with.

Essentially, the process of conveyancing lays down clear procedures for the conveyancer and also sets out each party's position during the sale or acquisition.

Before understanding the process of conveyancing, however, it is essential to understand something about the legal forms of ownership of property.

Legal ownership of property
There are two main forms of legal ownership of property in England and Wales. If you are about to embark on the sale or acquisition of a house or flat (or business) then you will be dealing in the main with either freehold or leasehold property. It is very rare indeed to find other forms of ownership, although, with the advent of the Commonhold and Leasehold Reform Act 2002, which became law in May 2002, the government

introduced a form of ownership called 'common hold' that in essence, creates the freehold ownership of flats, with common responsibility for communal areas.

Freehold property

In general, if you own the freehold of a house or a piece of land, then you will be the outright owner with no fixed period of time and no one else to answer to (with the exception of statutory authorities).

There may be registered restrictions on title, which we will be discussing later. The property will probably be subject to a mortgage so the only other overriding interest will be that of the bank or the building society. The responsibility for repairs, maintenance and general upkeep will be the freeholders. The law can intervene if certain standards are not maintained.

The deed to your house will be known as the "freehold transfer document" which will contain any rights and obligations. Usually, the transfer document will list any "Encumbrances" (restrictions) on the use of the land, such as rights of way of other parties, sales restrictions etc. The deeds to your home are the most important documentation. As we will see later, without deeds and historical data, such as the proof of title, it can be rather complicated selling property. This is why the system of land registration in use in this country has greatly simplified property transactions. Any person owning freehold property is free to create another interest in land, such as a lease or a weekly or monthly tenancy, subject to any restrictions the transfer may contain.

14

Leasehold property

If a person lives in a property owned by someone else and has an agreement for a period of time, usually a long period, over 21 years and up to 99 years or 125 years, and in some cases 999 years, then they are a leaseholder. The conveyancing of leasehold property is potentially, far more problematic than freehold property, particularly when the flat is in a block with a number of units.

The lease is a contract between landlord and tenant which lays down the rights and obligations of both parties and should be read thoroughly by both the leaseholder and, in particular, the conveyancer. Once signed then the purchaser is bound by all the clauses in the contract. It is worth looking at the nature of a lease before discussing the rather more complex process of conveyancing. Again, it has to be stated that it is of the utmost importance that both the purchaser and the vendor understand the nature of a lease.

The lease

Preamble

The start of a lease is called the preamble. This defines the landlord and purchaser and also the nature of the property in question (the demise). It will also detail the remaining period of the lease.

Leaseholders covenants

Covenants are best understood as obligations and responsibilities. Leaseholder's covenants are therefore a list of things that leaseholders should do, such as pay their service

15

charges and keep the interior of the dwelling in good repair and not, for example, to alter the structure. The landlord's covenants will set out the obligations of the landlord, which is usually to maintain the structure and exterior of the block and light common parts etc. One unifying theme of all leasehold property is that, notwithstanding the landlord's responsibilities, it is the leaseholder who will pay for everything out of a service charge.

Leases will make detailed provisions for the setting, managing and charging of service charges which should include a section on accounting. All landlords of leaseholders are accountable under the Landlord and Tenant Act 1985, as amended by the 1987 Act and the 2002 Commonhold and Leasehold Reform Act. These Acts will regulate the way a landlord treats a leaseholder in the charging and accounting of service charges.

In addition, the 1996 Housing Act and the Commonhold and Leasehold Reform Act 2002 have provided further legislation protecting leaseholders by introducing the rights of leaseholders to go to First Tier Tribunals (formerly Leasehold Valuation Tribunals) if they are unhappy with levels and management of charges and also to carry out audits of charges.

It is vital when buying a leasehold property that you read the lease. Leases tend to be different from each other and nothing can be assumed. When you buy a property, ensure that the person selling has paid all debts and has contributed to some form of "sinking fund" whereby provision has been built up for major repairs in the future. Make sure that you will not be landed with big bills after moving in and that if you are, there is money to deal with them. After a lease has been signed then there is little or no recourse to recoup any money owed.

These are all the finer points of leases and the conveyancer has to be very vigilant. In particular read the schedules to the lease as these sometimes contain rather more detail.

One of the main differences between leasehold and freehold property is that the lease is a long tenancy agreement which contains provisions that give the landlord rather a lot of power to manage (or mismanage) and it is always possibility that a leaseholder can be forced to give up his or her home in the event of non-compliance with the terms of the lease. This is known as forfeiture.

Under the Commonhold and Leasehold Reform Act 2002 referred to earlier, a 'no fault right to manage' was been introduced. This will enable leaseholders who are unhappy with the management of their property, to take over the management with relative ease. The Act apply to most landlords, with the exception of local authorities.

These powers go a long way to curb the excesses or inefficiencies of numerous landlords and will provide more control and greater security for leaseholders.

Check points
There are key areas of a lease that should be checked when purchasing. Some have already been discussed.

1) What is the term left on the lease?

2) Is the preamble clear, i.e. is the area which details landlord, tenant and demised (sold) premises clear?

3) Is the lease assignable, i.e. can you pass on the lease without landlords permission or does it need surrendering at sale or a license to assign?

4) What is the ground rent and how frequently will you pay it ?

5) What is the level of service charge, if any, and how is it collected, apportioned, managed and accounted for.

6) What are the general restrictions in the lease, can you have pets for example, can you park cars, do you have a designated space?

7) What are the respective repairing obligations?

As we have seen, the leaseholder will pay anyway but the landlord and leaseholder will hold respective responsibilities. This is an important point because occasionally, there is no stated responsibility for upkeep and the environment deteriorates as a consequence, diminishing the value of the property.

Business leases

Generally, the Landlord and Tenant Act 1954, part 2, provides the framework for those occupying premises on the basis of a business lease. There are a few exceptions to this such as mining leases and agricultural leases. The average business lease will be shorter than a residential lease and will contain periodic rent review clauses. The typical business lease may be for ten years with a rent review after the fifth year.

The whole process of conveyancing business leases, although similar to residential in some respect, is rather more complex. For example, maintenance rights and responsibilities are often an issue between the parties concerned and it is essential that there is a clear picture at the outset. Those coming to the end of the term of their leases can find themselves faced with a significant repair bill, based on a schedule of dilapidations undertaken by a surveyor.

As with all leases, it is very important to ensure that those managing have a firm and comprehensive grasp over the whole process. If they do not then this can affect the value of the property when you wish to sell or buy a lease. It is not advised that an individual undertakes this type of conveyancing, but employs a solicitor well versed in the finer points of business tenancies. 'A Straightforward Guide to Managing Commercial Property', deals with business tenancies in more depth.

Two systems of conveyancing

After gaining an understanding of the nature of the interest in land that you are buying, it is absolutely essential to understand the two systems of conveyancing property in existence, as this will determine, not so much the procedure because the initial basic steps in conveyancing, such as carrying out searches, are common to both forms of land, registered and unregistered, but the way you go about the process and the final registration.

Registered and Unregistered land

In England and Wales the method of conveyancing to be used in each particular transaction very much depends on whether the land is registered or unregistered land. If the title, or proof of ownership, of land and property has been registered under the Land Registration Acts 1925-86, as amended, then the Land Registry (see below) will be able to furnish the would-be conveyancer with such documentation as is required to establish ownership, or third party rights etc. If the land has not been registered then proof of ownership of the land in question must be traced through the title deeds.

Registered land

All conveyancing falls within the remit of the Land Registry, because it is compulsory to register land throughout England and Wales. The Land Registration Acts of 1925 established the Land Registry (HM land Registry). The Land Registry is a department of the Civil Service, at its head is the Chief Land Registrar. Anybody can obtain information which is held on the register of a registered title by going to www.landregistry-search.com. There is a list of fees on this site for various searches.

There is specific terminology in use within conveyancing, particularly within the Land Registry:

- A piece of land, or parcel of land is known as a registered title.
- The owner of land is referred to as the registered proprietor.
- A conveyance of registered land is called a transfer.
- A transaction involving registered land is known as a dealing.

The main difference between the two types of conveyancing, registered and unregistered concerns what is known as proof of title. In the case of land that is unregistered the owner will prove title by showing the would-be purchaser the documentary evidence which shows how he or she came to own the land and property.

In the case of registered land the owner has to show simply that he or she is registered at the Land Registry as the registered proprietor. Proof of registration is proof of ownership, which is unequivocal. In registered land the documents proving ownership are replaced by the fact of registration. Each separate title or ownership of land has a title number, which the Land Registry uses to trace or confirm ownership. The description of each title on the register is identified by the title number, described by reference to the filed plan (indicating limits and extent of ownership).

Production of the Land Certificate

Before the introduction of the Land Registration Act 2002, with registered land, whenever there is a sale, or disposition, then the Land Certificate had to be produced to the Land Registry in the appropriate district. The Land Registry no longer produces land or charge certificates.

Now read the key points from chapter 1 overleaf.

**

KEY POINTS FROM CHAPTER ONE

- Conveyancing is about how to transfer the ownership of land and property from one person to another.

- The process of conveyancing lays down clear procedures for the conveyancer and also sets out each party's position during the process.

- There are two systems of conveyancing-that dealing with registered land and that dealing with unregistered land. Proof of title is easier to establish when land is registered.

- It is compulsory throughout England and Wales to register land – in spite of this a significant amount of land remains unregistered.

**

KEY STEPS IN CONVEYANCING
THE INITIAL BASIC SEARCHES

Chapter 2

The Key Steps In The Process of Conveyancing Property-Basic Searches

---

Searches

In chapter's three and four, we will be looking specifically at the processes of conveyancing as they affect registered and unregistered land. However, before we do, it is necessary to look at the processes generally, in order to form a clear idea.

Before the buyer exchanges contracts on a property and then completes the purchase, a number of searches are always carried out. In this chapter we will be looking at four key searches:

- Enquiries before contract.
- Local land charges search.
- Enquiries of the local authority.
- Index map search

These are the most essential and common searches and a number of the searches are carried out by the seller. Most searches today can be carried out online, for which there is a fee. You should first go to the relevant local authority web page.

Enquiries before contract

There are inquiries to the seller, or the vendor of the property and are aimed at revealing certain facts about the property that the seller has no legal obligation to disclose to the buyer. There are certain matters which are always raised. These are:

- Whether there are any existing boundary disputes.
- What services are supplied to the property, whether electricity, gas or other.
- Any easements or covenants in the lease. These are stipulations in the lease which give other certain rights, such as right of way.
- Any guarantees in existence.
- Planning considerations..
- Adverse rights affecting the property.
- Any fixtures and fittings.
- Whether there has been any breach of restriction affecting the property.

The seller's property information forms

If the property is newly built, information will be required concerning any outstanding works and of future guarantees of remedying defects. Where a property is leasehold, information will be required about the lessor.

Registered conveyancers will use a standard form to raise these enquiries, so that the initial search is exhaustive. As part of the move towards openness in the process of buying and selling property, and also an attempt to speed up the process of sale, the Law Society introduced forms which the solicitor, or buyer if

26

carrying out his or her own conveyancing, is being encouraged to use. These are Seller's Property Information Form TA6 and TA7 for leasehold information (if leasehold). Requisition on title forms are also used. The Law Society Website will give information on what forms are currently used in addition to the aforementioned. These forms can be obtained from a legal stationers, such as Oyez or, in most cases, from the Land Registry website.

Answers given by the vendor do not form part of the subsequent contract and therefore cannot be used against that person in the event of future problems. However, the Misrepresentations Act of 1976 could be evoked if a deliberate misrepresentation has caused problems.

Local land charge search

The Local Land Charge Act 1975 requires District Councils, London Borough Councils and the City of London Corporation to maintain a Local Land Charges Registry for the area. However, you should note changes being introduced.

Full details can be obtained from:

www.gov.uk/government/publications/local-land-charges/local-land-charges.

These changes relate to the future role of the Land Registry when making searches. Local land charges can be divided into two areas:

- Financial charges on the land for work carried out by the local authority.
- Restrictions on the use of land.

The register is further divided into twelve parts:
- General financial charges.
- Specific financial charges.
- Planning charges.
- Miscellaneous charges and provisions.
- Charges for improvements of ways over fenland.
- Land compensation charges.
- New town charges.
- Civil aviation charges.
- Open cast coal mining charges.
- Listed buildings charges.
- Light obstruction notices.
- Drainage scheme charges.

All charges are enforceable by the local authority except g and i, which are enforced by statutory bodies and private individuals generally.

A buyer should search in all parts of this particular register and this can be done by a personal or official search. A personal search, as the name suggests, involves the individual or their agent attending at the local authority office, and on paying the relevant fee, personally searching the register. The charges are registered against the land concerned and not against the owner. The official search is the one most favoured because, in the event of missing a vital piece of information the chances of compensation are far higher than with a personal search.

With the official search a requisition for a search and for an official certificate of search is sent to the Register of Local Land Charges for the area within which the land is situated. There is a fee and the search is carried out by the Registrars staff, which results in a certificate being sent to the person making the request, which clearly outlines any charges. The Registrar may require a plan of the land as well as the postal address. Separate searches are made of each parcel of land being purchased.

Local authority enquiries

There are two parts to a local authority search – a LLC1 and a CON29. The LLC1 – Local Land Charge Register search – covers any charges or attendant restrictions relating to land or property.

These can include whether the property is:
- a listed building
- located in a conservation area
- subject to a tree protection order
- in need of an improvement or renovation grant
- or situated in a smoke control zone

The form also covers planning agreements and conditional planning permissions. All LLC1 registrations are legally binding on successive owners. The second part of the search – the CON29 – supplies information relating to public highways, proposals for new roads, rail schemes or planning decisions that could affect the property, as well as outstanding statutory notices, breaches of planning or building regulations or the existence of a compulsory purchase order. Environmental factors, such as whether the house stands on contaminated land or in a Radon gas affected area are also covered.

The standard forms in use contain a statement to the effect that the local authority is not responsible for errors unless negligence is proved. Many of the inquiries relate specifically to planning matters, whilst other elements of the search are concerned about roads and whether they are adopted and whether there are likely to be ant costs falling onto property owners.

We will be considering planning matters concerning the individual property a little later. Other inquiries relate to possible construction of new roads which may effect the property, the location of sewers and pipes and whether the property is in an area of compulsory registration of title, a smoke controlled area or slum clearance area. The form used is so constructed that part 2 of the form contains questions, which must be initialled by the purchaser before they are answered.

Again these questions cover planning and other matters. Other enquiries can be made by the individual, which are answered at the authorities discretion. In addition to the above, which are the major searches, there are others that the conveyancer has to be aware of.

These are as follows:

Searches in the Index map and parcels index of the Land Register

If the land has been registered the title will be disclosed and whether it is registered, leasehold or freehold. Registered rent charges are also disclosed by the search.

Commons Registration Act (1965) search

This act imposes a duty on county councils to keep a register relating to village greens and common land and interests over them, such as right of way.

Coal mining search

The request for this search if relevant, is designed to reveal the whereabouts of mineshafts and should be sent to the local area coal board office, or its equivalent. The search will disclose past workings and any subsidence, proposed future workings and the proximity of opencast workings. It is usually well known if there is a problem, or potential problem with coal mining in an area and this search is essential if that is the case.

Other enquiries

There are a number of other bodies from which it might be appropriate to request a search. These include British Rail, Statutory undertakers such as electricity, water and gas boards, planning authorities generally, rent assessment committees and so on.

These will only be necessary if there is a direct link between the property being purchased and a particular circumstance within an area or property.

Chancel searches

Chancel repair search – to ensure there are no potential leftover medieval liabilities on the property to help pay for church repairs. This is a necessity and costs £20. However, you may decide to take out Chancel repair insurance instead for £20 or so. The laws around Chancel repair changed in October 2013 so now the onus is on the Church to establish and lodge liability with the Land Registry.

Planning matters relating to specific properties

It is obviously very necessary to determine whether or not any illegal alterations have been carried out to the property you wish to purchase, before reaching the point of exchange of contracts. This is to ensure that the vendor has complied with relevant planning legislation, if any material changes have been made, and that you will not be required at a later date to carry out remedial work. The local authority maintains a register of planning applications relating to properties within their boundaries. In addition, the register will also reveal any planning enforcement notices in force against a particular property.

Questions such as these, and also any questions relating to the effect of structure or local plans, (specific plans relating to local and borough wide plans for the future) should be made in writing to the local authority or an individual search can be carried out. Usually they are carried out if there is any suspicion that planning regulations may have been breached. In addition, there may be other considerations, such as whether the building is listed or whether tree preservation orders relating to trees within the curtilage of the property are in force. It is certainly essential to know about these.

It is highly recommended that all of these searches are carried out and completed before contracts are exchanged.

Environmental searches

Environmental Searches – this report is used on the vast majority of transactions and is provided by either Landmark or Groundsure. Depending which product your solicitor usually uses, the report will give information about contaminated land at or around the property, landfill sites, former and current industry, detailed flooding predictions, radon gas hazard, ground stability issues, and some other related information. The cost should be around £50 to £60 including VAT.

Optional and specific locational searches

Optional and location specific searches – sometimes extra searches are required or recommended depending on the location or type of property or due to particular concerns raised by the buyer. These could include:

- -
- Tin Mining searches in Cornwall.
- Mining searches in various parts of the UK and Cheshire Brine searches
- Additional Local Authority Questions such as Public Paths, Pipelines, Noise Abatement Zones, Common Land, etc.

Now read the key points from chapter two.

KEY POINTS FROM CHAPTER TWO

- Before the buyer exchanges contracts on a property it is essential to carry out a number of key searches.

- In addition to the main search, there are a number of ancillary searches which should be made if appropriate.

- There are standard forms for carrying out such searches-if you are doing your own conveyancing these can be obtained from any legal stationers.

- There may be other considerations such as conservation or planning issues that need to be looked into.

**

Chapter 3

THE STUCTURAL SURVEY – The National House Builders Council (Buildmark)

Anyone who purchases a property should carry out a structural survey. This is highly advisable and preferably should be as in-depth as possible. A chartered surveyor should be used. If a qualified surveyor is negligent when compiling his or her report of the property then that person can be sued. Most residential property is purchased with assistance from a building society or bank. The lender will insist on a survey before lending the money in order to protect their advance. However, this survey is cursory at the best and will not reveal more serious problems. Therefore, at this point in the conveyancing process, the person purchasing, or the person acting on his or her behalf should ensure that they are thoroughly acquainted with the condition of the property. If you are purchasing a house which is in the course of construction, then there will be the benefit of a warranty of good work and proper materials so that the house will be fit for habitation. This protection does not extend to any subsequent purchases. There is however, a form of statutory protection under the Defective Premises Act of 1972 which imposes a duty on a developer and those associated with the developer to build in a correct manner. The Act covers anyone acquiring an interest in a dwelling.

The National House Builders Scheme

This scheme was redrafted in 1979 and, in 1988, the Buildmark scheme was introduced. Builders who are registered with the NHBS must offer a warranty to first and subsequent purchasers, that, essentially, has a ten-year shelf life from date of construction.

During the first two years from issue the builder is liable to make good any defects due to non-compliance with NHBS regulations. The first two years are known as the initial guarantee period. After this, the remaining eight years are referred to as the structural guarantee period. During this time the NHBS will reimburse the purchaser the cost of remedying major works caused by any defect in the structure or subsidence, settlement or heave, provided that there is no other insurance at the time of the claim to cover the cost.

Liability of the builder outside the two year period

The NHBS agreement states that if any work undertaken by the builder in the initial guarantee period to remedy a defect caused by the breach of the NHBS requirements fails to remedy the defect or damage, the vendor/builder will remain under a continuing liability to remedy the damage after the initial guarantee period. Conveyancing a property is not just about successfully reaching a conclusion in a sale. It is also about ensuring that the property you are buying is sound and that you make sure that you have a clear picture of what you are buying, preferably by obtaining a report from a chartered surveyor.

Now read the key points from chapter three.

KEY POINTS FROM CHAPTER THREE

- Anyone who purchases a property must carry out a structural survey. It is essential that a qualified surveyor is used.

- If you are purchasing a house under construction there will be the benefit of a warranty with the property.

- The National Builders Scheme offers a warranty for ten years for those who purchase a house/flat from a registered developer.

**

PROOF OF TITLE AND OTHER SEARCHES—UNREGISTERED LAND AND REGISTERED LAND

Chapter 4

Conveyancing Unregistered land

We have considered the processes of conveyancing generally and the searches common to all property. However, it is now necessary to look at the specifics of conveyancing registered and unregistered land.

With unregistered land, as we have seen, there is a duty on the vendor to prove his or her title to the land, i.e., that they own the land in question. If all is registered at the Land Registry then life can be a good deal simpler. However, if not, then the process can be more complex.

The abstract of title – unregistered land. Establishing proof of ownership

The Abstract of title is an epitome of the various documents and events which together demonstrate that the vendor has good title to the land, conclusively owns the land. The vendor must, at his or her own expense, produce and deliver a proper abstract of title to the purchaser, unless there is an agreement to do otherwise, which would be unusual.

The abstract starts with the root or the origin of title. Every deed which dealt with transactions relating to this property subsequently must be abstracted. A conveyance relating to the purchase of the freehold is the strongest form of root of title, likewise a mortgage deed relating to that conveyance. If a vendor has lost any of the titles which relate to the land then it is usual for the vendor to insert a special condition into the contract stating what secondary evidence will be produced to prove title. Secondary evidence can be in the form of a counterpart lease, for example.

Once the abstract has been delivered, the purchaser must examine these documents against the originals. The purpose of the examination is to ensure that what has been abstracted has been properly or correctly abstracted, ensure that each document has been properly executed, attested and stamped and that there have been no changes to the title, such as memoranda endorsed on deeds or documents. Any doubt as to the validity of the title should be raised with the vendor's solicitor directly and promptly by written requisition. The purchaser is entitled to raise requisitions on any part of the title which is unsatisfactory, for example, if the title discloses a mortgage or covenant which was not disclosed in the contract. An omission from the abstract may be remedied by an answer to the requisition. The expense of verification of this answer is the purchaser's. The purchaser can serve a notice on the vendor requiring him to furnish an answer by a given date. Failure to reply by this date entitles the purchaser to rescind the contract. If the purchaser is still not satisfied with the vendor's replies, he or she can send observations back to the vendor relating to the reply.

There is a standard condition of sale, which states that the vendor can rescind the sale if he or she cannot furnish a reasonable reply to the requisition. This right however, is based on reasonable grounds, i.e., inability or unwillingness to answer.

Pre-completion searches

We discussed the key searches to be carried out prior to exchange and completion in the previous chapter. There are, however, other searches necessary, depending on the status of the property. With unregistered property, some of these searches involve the land Registry.

The purchaser or agent should carry out various searches immediately before completion in order to determine whether there are any encumbrances affecting the vendor's title to the property. The most important of these is the Land Charge Register of the Land Charge Department of the Land Registry.

HM Land Registry is working in partnership with local authorities in England to standardise and migrate local land charges register information to one accessible place.

Every local authority in England, with the exception of county councils, is required to hold a local land charges register that records obligations affecting properties within their administrative area. Under the Infrastructure Act 2015 responsibility for the 316 registers was transferred to HM Land Registry in a phased approach beginning in summer of 2018.

Anyone can access their new Local Land Charges service through their Search for local land charges service. Business customers can also access it through their portal accounts or Business Gateway. Each search result provides details of entries on the Local Land Charges Register relating to the land or property concerned.

Local authorities will continue to provide replies to CON29 enquiries, such as nearby road schemes or outstanding notices, which may affect a purchaser's decision whether to proceed. Once a local authority's local land charges data has been migrated to HM Land Registry, you will no longer be able to get local land charge search results from that local authority.

Using their new service, you will have the option of downloading a personal search for free or an official search for £15. Alternatively, you can use a search provider who will access the Local Land Charges service for you.

This is a historic step forward in the Government's ambition to make the home-buying process simpler, faster and cheaper. It is also an important part of their Business Strategy to help improve the entire conveyancing process.

Methods of making a land charge search

A search may be made in person, by post, by telephone or online (the preferred method). Information required for a postal search is the name of the estate owner, period of years searched against, address, county and description of property. Completed searches are usually sent back promptly. If the search reveals an adverse entry then the purchaser should ensure that the property concerned is not affected.

Other searches

Company searches are usually necessary if the property to be purchased is from a company. Company agents can ascertain whether there is a winding up order against the company or whether there are any specific charges relating to that company registered against the title to land.

The nature of the conveyance

It should be noted that if land to be conveyed is in an area of compulsory registration at the Land Registry, as most land is, the purchasers solicitor may, instead of preparing the traditional form of conveyance as described below, utilises the much simpler form of a registered land transfer. For those whose property will not be immediately registered the following applies:

The purchaser's solicitor will prepare a draft conveyance in duplicate and send it to the vendor's solicitor for scrutiny and approval. The vendor's solicitor will normally send back a copy with amendments in red pen. When the deed is agreed (settled) the purchaser's solicitor has it engrossed (fair copied) and then sends it to the vendor's solicitor to keep until the day of completion.

The contents of a typical conveyance of unregistered land

An example conveyance is shown further on in this chapter. The heading of the document will begin with the words "This conveyance" or "This deed of gift " etc. The conveyance is dated and the full names of the parties are inserted along with their addresses. If there are parties other than the vendor and purchaser, for example, any trustees, they are also inserted.

The Recital

This part of the deed will usually begin "whereas" and the purpose is to outline a history of transactions related to that property. They are largely unnecessary and are there as a result of tradition as it has evolved in conveyancing.

The Testatum

The Testatum is part of the operative part of the conveyance and will begin with "Now this deed witnesses".

The formal words are followed by a statement of consideration for the transaction and a receipt by the vendor for the purchase money. No other receipt is required, although this does not stop a vendor challenging the fact that a receipt has been paid.

Words of grant

These are the words that pass the vendor's estate to the purchaser. The usual form of words will state "The vendor as beneficial owner hereby conveys." There will then be a description of the property conveyed, known as the parcels clause.

In a lease there will be what is known as a reddendum, which goes on to describe rent and rent days. There are also what is known as covenants, either negative or positive covenants,

46

which impose obligations, or rights on either party. In modern developments these conveyances are usually very lengthly and are contained in a schedule to the deed.

Where a vendor remains liable on a covenant after sale he or she should ensure that the purchaser enters into a covenant to indemnify the vendor in respect of any liability arising from a future breach of that covenant. The effect is to indemnify the vendor against any loss or expenses in respect of breach of covenant. Where the property is conveyed to joint tenants a clause is very often included declaring that each tenant holds joint equity and conferring on the co-owners additional powers of dealing with the land in question.

The Testimonium

This is the formal clause, which precedes the party's execution of the deed and will typically be worded " In witness where of the parties here to have executed this document as their deed the day and year first before mentioned".

Execution of deeds before July 31st 1990

The Law of Property Act 1989 introduced very important changes in the execution of deeds. Under the Law of Property Act 1925 three formal requirements for a deed are outlined, namely that it must be signed sealed and delivered. The effective date of the deed is the effective date of delivery. However, after 1989 a seal is no longer required, just an effective signature, signed before a witness. The Companies Act 1989 also allows for companies to execute a deed by signature, with a seal no longer a requirement.

Completion of sale of unregistered land

The date for completion will be stated in the contract. See chapter 6. Usually, completion will take place at the offices of the vendor's solicitor. If there is an outstanding mortgage on the property and the mortgagee will not release the deeds to the vendor's solicitor until after it is discharged then completion will take place at the mortgagees solicitor. Completion allows for settling of the financial account between vendor and purchaser and completion of legal work plus handing over the executed deed. Money is usually sent from a bank to the solicitor. Deeds are usually examined a last time to see that all is correct. The vendor may retain part of a title deed if there is any ongoing involvement, i.e., part ownership of land etc.

In unregistered conveyancing the legal estate is vested in the purchaser. The purchaser is also entitled to possession of the property and the solicitors should ensure that adequate arrangements have been made to this end. Where the vendor is selling as a personal representative of another, a memoranda of sale should be endorsed on the grant of representation which he or she will have. Where the purchaser enters into covenants for the protection of land retained or is granted additional rights, such as rights over land, it is common for the vendor to retain a duplicate copy (counterpart).

Example of conveyance of unregistered land overleaf.

This CONVEYANCE BY DEED is made the day of 20**** between J Smith of 19 Jupiter Street, Othertown (hereinafter called the vendor) of one part and F Deal of 1 Mars Street Eithertown (hereinafter called the purchaser) of the other part.

WHEREAS

……………

The vendor is seised of the property hereinafter described for an estate in fee simple in possession free from encumbrances and as hereinafter mentioned and has agreed with the purchaser for the sale to him of the said property for a like estate for a price of Seventy five thousand pounds

………………………………

NOW THIS DEED WITNESSETH

…………In pursuance of the said agreement and in consideration of the sum of seventy five thousand pounds now paid hereby acknowledges the vendor as beneficial owner hereby conveys Otherplace, Othertown as was conveyed to the vendor by John Rarer by conveyance of 25th May 1952 and is further therein more particularly described and subject to the covenants therein contained but otherwise free from encumbrances TO HOLD the same unto the purchaser in fee simple

---

With the object and intent of affording to the vendor a full and sufficient indemnity but not further or otherwise the purchaser hereby covenants with the vendor to observe and perform the above mentioned covenant and to indemnify the vendor against all actions claims demands and liabilities in respect thereof ……

It is hereby certified that the transaction affected does not form part of a larger transaction or of a series of transactions in respect of which the amount or value or the aggregate amount or value of the consideration exceeds eighty pounds ....

IN WITNESS whereof the parties hereto have executed this document as their deed the day and year first before written.

EXECUTED AS HIS DEED

By the aforementioned

J Smith in the presence of   ) J Smith

K Knowles

46 hilltop

Otherplace

EXECUTED AS HIS DEED

By the aforementioned

John Rarer in the presence of   ) J Rarer

K Smile

Child Street

Cidertown   )

Now read the key points from chapter four.

**

KEY POINTS FROM CHAPTER FOUR

- The purchasers solicitor will prepare a draft in conveyance in duplicate and send in duplicate to the vendors solicitor for scrutiny and approval.

- When the deal is agreed, the purchaser's solicitor has it engrossed and the sends it to the vendor's solicitor until completion.

- Deeds executed after July 31st 1990 do not require a seal.

- The date for completion should be clearly stated in the contract.

- Completion allows for the settling of the financial account between vendor and purchaser.

**

Chapter 5

Conveyancing Registered Land

In chapter four, we looked at the general process of conveyancing unregistered land. In this chapter we will concentrate on registered land. In all likelihood, you will be dealing with registered land as most property is now registered.

First Registration of title

Note:

Practice introduced on 28 November 2016:

Conveyancers can lodge certified copy deeds and documents instead of originals, provided they meet certain conditions.

First registration of land may take place voluntarily or compulsorily depending on the nature of the transaction. Land Registry form FR1 should be used. Compulsory registration now extends to most of England and Wales. It is highly undesirable to complete a sale of land and then neglect to register it.

When a sale is completed an application must be lodged for registration within two months of completion. The effect of non-registration is that the deed of transfer, or the conveyance, becomes null and void after the two-month period. In other words, there is no choice but to register the land.

Under s123 of the Law of Property Act, the Chief Land Registrar may accept a late registration. An explanation of why the property was not registered within the time period will be required. Acceptance of the application has the effect of registering the estate to the purchaser from the date of completion. Late applications are rarely refused. When land is purchased in a compulsory area but the title is not yet registered, even where the transaction must be followed by a first registration the procedure until completion is identical to the procedure in unregistered conveyancing.

The purchaser's solicitor will forward the correct form to the land registry. This form is called a "cover" because it is double sided and when folded will contain all the necessary documentation for registration. The cover will contain a certificate signed by a solicitor that the title has been properly investigated, a statement that any land charges entries revealed by the official search either do or do not effect the land concerned and if they do a note of the document by which they were created. In addition, a schedule of encumbrances affecting the property is sent.

All the original deeds and other documents of title must be sent. Enough information by way of plan must be sent to enable registry staff to fix the position of the property on the Ordnance Survey Map. There is a prescribed fee which the Land Registry can provide details of on request.

For application by the owner for first registration of leasehold land other than on the grant of a new lease and for application

54

by the owner for first registration of leasehold land on grant of a new lease, there are different forms in use.

Outline of the registration process

In registered land the documents of title are replaced by the fact of registration. Therefore, the equivalent to the title deed is the various entries in the Land Registry.

Each title is given a title number, which is then used to trace title. The description of each title is identified by a title number, described by reference to a filed plan and a set of index cards retained to record specifics about that title.

The index cards and the filed plan are the equivalent of title deeds. The registered proprietor is issued with a land certificate containing a facsimile copy of the registered title. If land within a particular title number is subject to a mortgage the land certificate is retained by the Registry and the mortgagee is instead issued with a charge certificate, and the land certificate is retained by the Land Registry.

There are three registers of title at the Land Registry, the Property Register, The Proprietorship Register and The Charges Register.

The Property Register is similar to the Parcel Clause in unregistered conveyancing i.e., it describes the land in question. It will identify the geographical location and extent of the registered property by means of a short description and a reference to an official plan, which is prepared for each title. It

55

may also give particulars of any rights that benefit the land, for example, a right of way over adjoining land. In the case of a lease the register will also describe the parties to the lease, the term and the rent, any exceptions or reservations from the lease and, if the lessors title is registered, the title number.

The Proprietorship Register is similar to the Habendum in unregistered conveyancing. It will describe the type of title, i.e., title absolute, leasehold etc, the full name and address of the registered proprietor, description of that person, date of registration, price paid for the property and any other relevant entries. There will also be any relevant cautions, inhibitions or restrictions entered on the Register.

The Charges Register contains any encumbrance affecting the registered property, such as mortgages and any other charges taken over the property. However, details of the amount of money involved are not disclosed.

How to inspect the Register

The Land Registry has an online conveyancing system. Normally, solicitors use this and evidence of title can be deduced by going on to the web site. Evidence of title can also be obtained by writing to the Land Registry. If you wish, after you have received the copies of the register that you require, you can, by filling in the appropriate forms, obtain copies of documents that you would like to inspect. Again, a fee is payable. If you only wish to know the name and address of the registered proprietor of a property, you should fill in Land Registry form PN1.

You should then phone the Land Registry Customer Support Team on 0300 006 0411 or email at:

customersupport@landregistry.gov.uk They will direct you to the relevant office to send the form to.

The Land/Charge Certificate
Prior to 2003, when a title was registered for the first time or changed hands, a Land Certificate was issued by the Land Registry. The Land Certificate was regarded as the equivalent to the title deed although this can be misleading as it is only a facsimile of the official register and may not be up to date. In addition, there may be matters of title not contained on the register.

As mentioned in the introduction, following the introduction of the Land Registration Act 2002, and the practice of 'Dematerialisation' Land and Charge Certificates have now been abolished. If you have lost your certificate you do not need to replace it. Electronic copies of the land certificate can now be obtained through the Land Registry website.

Maps and descriptions of land
The Index map and parcels index provides that a map should be kept showing the position and extent of all registered titles. This is called the Public Index Map. This is open to inspection by any person, and can be inspected personally or by official search. There will be a fee for this search. All registered land must, in addition, be described by the applicant in such a way as to enable the land to be fully identified on the ordnance map or

general map. The Land Registry uses a consistent colour coding on its plans. This does not vary and it is expected that solicitors when preparing plans will use the same system. The colouring scheme is as follows:

- Red edging marks the extent of land within a particular title.
- Green tinting shows excluded pieces of land within the area of the title.
- Brown tinting shows land over which the registered land has a right of way.
- Blue tinting shows land within the title subject to a right of way.

For further references, colours are used in the following order:

- Tinting in pink, blue yellow and mauve.
- Edging with a blue yellow or mauve band.
- Hatching with a colour other than black or green.
- Numbering or lettering of small self contained areas.

In addition, when reading a filed plan it should be noted that a boundary represented by a feature shown on the ground or on the existing ordnance survey is represented by a continuous dark line. A boundary not representing such a feature is shown by a broken dark line. The scale of the filed plan is usually 1/1250 enlarged from the survey 1/2500.

Now read the key points from chapter five.

KEY POINTS FROM CHAPTER FIVE

- Registered conveyancing entails the owner simply demonstrating that the registered proprietorship is recorded at the Land Registry.

- Each title is given a title number, which is described by reference to a filed plan and set of Index Cards. These are the equivalent of title deeds.

- There are three registers of title at the Land Registry, The Property Register, The Proprietorship Registry and The Charges Register.

- First registration of land may take place voluntarily or be compulsory depending on the nature of the transaction.

**

THE CONTRACT FOR SALE – EXCHANGE AND COMPLETION

Chapter 6

The Contract For Sale

Forming the contract

Having discussed the processes involved in conveying registered and unregistered land, prior to exchange and completion, it is now necessary to look at the contract for sale, which is formulated at the outset but not exchanged or completed before all parties are satisfied with the prior processes of conveyancing.

As with many other transactions, a sale of land is effected through a contract. However, a contract which deals with the sale of land is governed by the requirements of the Law of Property (miscellaneous provisions) Act 1989, the equitable doctrine of specific performance and the duty of the vendor to provide title to the property.

The Law of Property Act (miscellaneous provisions) 1989 provides that contracts dealing with the sale of land after 26th September 1989 must be in writing. The contract must contain all the terms and agreements to which the respective parties to the transaction have agreed. The provisions of the Act do not apply to sales at a public auction, contracts to grant a short lease and contracts regulated under the Financial Services Act 1986. If the person purchasing is doing so through an agent then the agent must have authority to act on behalf of the purchaser. Example of agents are auctioneers, solicitors and estate agents.

Agreements

If the phrase "subject to contract" is used in a sale then the intention of both parties to the contract is that neither are contractually bound until a formal contract has been agreed by the parties, signed and exchanged. Therefore, the words "subject to contract" are a protective device, although it is not good to depend on the use of these words throughout a transaction.

Procedures in the formation of contract

The vendor's solicitor will usually draw up an initial contract of sale. This is because only this person has access to all the necessary initial documents to begin to effect a contract. The draft contract is prepared in two parts and sent to the purchaser's solicitor (if using a solicitor) and the other side will approve or amend the contract as necessary. Both sides must agree to any proposed amendments. (see standard letters used in process of conveyancing appendix 1). After agreement has been reached, the vendor's solicitor will retain one copy of the contract and send the other copy to the solicitor or person acting for the other side. The next stage is for the vendor's solicitor to engross (sign and formalise) the contract in two parts. Both parts are the sent to the purchaser's solicitor or other agent who checks that they are correct then sends one part back to the vendor's solicitor.

Signing the contract

The vendor's solicitor will obtain the vendor's signature to the contract, when he is satisfied that the vendor can sell what he is purporting to do through the contract. The purchaser's solicitor or agent will do the same, having checked the replies to all inquiries before contract. It is also essential to check that a mortgage offer has been made and accepted.

Signing the Transfer

The transfer form TR1 is the document transferring ownership of the property to the buyer. It confirms the details set out in the contract. The transfer is sent out by the solicitor (see standard letters appendix 1) for you to sign in readiness for exchange and completion.

Exchanging contracts

Neither party to the sale is legally bound until there has been an exchange of contracts. At one time, a face-to-face exchange would have taken place. However, with the rapid increases in property transactions this rarely happens nowadays. Exchange by post or telephone is more common.

The purchaser will post his or her part of the contract together with the appropriate cheque, or bank transfer, to cover the agreed deposit to the purchaser's solicitor or person acting on behalf of that person. The deposit is usually 10% of the purchase price although there are variations on this theme. The amounts are agreed between buyer and seller. The purchaser's solicitor will usually insert the agreed completion date. On receiving this part of the contract the vendor will add his or her part and send this off in exchange. At this stage, both parties become bound under the contract.

The Contents of a contract

A contract will be in two parts, the particulars of sale and the conditions of sale. The particulars of sale give a physical description of the land and also of the interest which is being sold. A property must be described accurately and a plan may be attached to the contract to emphasise or illustrate what is in the contract. The particulars will also outline whether the property is freehold or leasehold and what kind of lease the vendor is assigning, i.e., Head lease (where vendor is owner of the freehold) or Underlease, (where the vendor is not).

It is very important to determine what kind of lease it is that is being assigned, indeed whether it is assignable or whether permission is needed from the landlord and it is recommended that a solicitor handle this transaction. This is because any purchaser of a lease can find his or her interest jeopardised by the nature of the lease. Where a sub-lease, or under lease is being purchased, the purchasers interest can be forfeited by the actions of the head lessee, the actions of this person being out of control of the purchaser.

Rights, such as easements and also restrictive covenants, which are for the benefit of the land, should be expressly referred to in the particulars of sale. In addition, the vendor should refer to any latent defects affecting his or her property, if known. This includes any encumbrances, which may affect the property.

Miss-description

If the property in the particulars of sale is described wrongly, i.e., there is a misstatement of fact, such as describing leasehold as freehold land, calling an under-lease a lease or leaving out something that misleads the buyer, in other words, if the mis-description is material, then the purchaser is entitled to rescind the contract. Essentially the contract must describe what is being sold and if it does not, and the buyer is mislead then the contract is inaccurate.

If the miss-description is immaterial and insubstantial, and there has been no misrepresentation then the purchaser cannot rescind the contract. However, if the miss-description has affected the purchase price of the property then the purchaser can insist on a reduction in the asking price. The purchaser should claim this compensation before completion takes place.

The vendor has no right to rescind the contract if the miss-description is in the purchaser's favour, for example, the area of land sold is greater than that intended. Neither can the vendor compel the purchaser to pay an increased purchase price.

Misrepresentation

Misrepresentation is an untrue statement of fact made by one party or his or her agent, which induces the other party to enter into the contract. An opinion and a statement of intention must be distinguished from a statement of fact. There are three types of misrepresentation and innocent misrepresentation. Fraudulent misrepresentation is a false statement made knowingly or without belief in its truth, or recklessly.

67

The innocent party may sue through the tort of negligence either before or after the contract is complete and rescind the contract. Negligent misrepresentation, although not fraudulent, is where the vendor or his or her agents cannot prove that the statement they made in relation to the contract was correct. Remedies available are damages or rescission of the contract. Innocent misrepresentation is where the statement made was neither fraudulently or negligently but is still an untrue statement. Rescission is available for this particular type of misrepresentation. Rescission of contract generally is available under the Misrepresentation Act 1967s 2 (2).

Non-disclosure
Generally, in the law of contract, there is the principle of "caveat emptor" "let the buyer beware". In other words, it is up to the purchaser to ensure that what he or she is buying is worth the money paid for it. Earlier we talked about the importance of searches and also, particularly, the importance of the structural survey. Although the vendor has some responsibility to reveal any defects in the property it is always very advisable for the purchaser to ensure that all checks prior to purchase are carried out thoroughly.

Conditions of sale
There are two types of conditions, special conditions and general conditions. Special conditions are those which are specific to an individual contract, such as when a specific day is fixed for completion. The general conditions are those which have general application. General conditions of sale are standard entitled, "National protocol for domestic leasehold and freehold

property". This is a complete guide to conveyancing in itself and can be obtained from the Law Society. The Law Society has recently updated this protocol.

The general conditions of sale oblige the vendor to supply the purchaser with abstracts or any copies of a lease or agreement in writing. The vendor must always supply the purchaser with details of any tenancy agreements in existence. A deposit for the purchase will only be payable if there is a special or general condition to this effect, such a term is not implied into a contract. Under standard conditions a deposit of 10 percent of the purchase price is paid to the vendor's solicitor prior to purchase but this can be varied between parties. The deposit should be paid by Bank Transfer at the date of the contract (exchange). Failure to pay, or payment by a cheque, which is subsequently dishonoured, is a breach and can lead to the vendor rescinding the contract. The general conditions specifically refer to this.

If there is any interest due, or expected on purchase money this will be dealt with in the special conditions of contract.

Completion

The requirements concerning completion are detailed thoroughly in the general conditions of sale. Payment on completion is one such detail. Payment on completion should be by bank transfer.

At common law, completion takes place whenever the vendor wishes and payment is to be made by legal tender. Also dealt with in the general conditions is failure to complete and notice to complete. Failure to complete can cause difficulty for one of the other parties and the aggrieved party can serve notice on the other to complete by a specific date. The notice has the effect of making "time of the essence" which means that a specific date is attached to completion, after which the contract is discharged.

Return of deposit

The vendor must return any deposit if the purchaser drops out before the exchange of contracts. This cannot be prevented and was the subject of a House of Lords ruling in the 1977 case Sorrel v Finch.

The position of the parties after exchange of contracts

Once a contract has been exchanged the purchaser is the beneficial owner of the property, with the vendor owning the property on trust for the purchaser. The vendor is entitled to any rents or other profits from the land during this period, and has the right to retain the property until final payments have been made and has a lien (charge/ right) over the property in respect of any unpaid purchase monies.

The vendor is bound to take reasonable care of the property and should not let the property fall into disrepair or other damages to be caused during the period between exchange and completion. If completion does not take place at the allotted time and the fault is the purchasers then interest can be charged on the money due. The purchaser, as beneficial owner of the property is entitled to any increase in the value of the land and buildings but not profits arising. The purchaser has a right of lien
70

over the property, the same as the vendor, in respect of any part of the purchase price prior to completion.

Bankruptcy of the vendor

In the unfortunate event of the vendor going bankrupt in between exchange and completion. The normal principles of bankruptcy apply so that the trustee in bankruptcy steps in to the vendor's shoes. The purchaser can be compelled to complete the sale. The trustee in bankruptcy is obliged to complete the sale if the purchaser tenders the purchase money on the completion day.

Bankruptcy of the purchaser

When a purchaser is declared bankrupt in between sale and completion, all of his or her property vests in the trustee in bankruptcy. The trustee can compel the vendor to complete the transaction by paying monies due by the allotted day. If the vendor wishes to proceed with the sale and the trustee is reluctant, the trustee has the right to claim that the contract is onerous. However, in these circumstances, the vendor can keep any deposit due to him.

Death of the vendor or the purchaser

The personal representatives of a deceased vendor can compel the purchaser to sell. The money is conveyed to those representatives who will hold the money in accordance with the terms of any will or in accordance with the rules relating to intestacy if there is no will. The same position applies to the purchaser's representatives, who can be compelled by the vendor to complete the purchase and who can hold money on the purchaser's behalf.

Other factors in the conveyancing process

Obtaining proof of identity

Solicitors are obliged by law to obtain evidence of those who intend to sell or purchase property. This is in line with regulations published in the Council of Mortgage Lenders Handbook-dealing with money laundering. The documents supplied (listed below) have to be certified either by a solicitor or the estate agent dealing with the sale. The post office can also verify the documents for a small fee. You will need to prove identification and address.

Proof of identity. This can be your passport or photo card driving licence. A copy may be acceptable if it is certified as a true likeness by a regulated person.

Proof of address

This can be a utility bill less than three months old, a council tax demand or bank statement. The solicitor in question will supply you with a list of acceptable documents.

Cash is not acceptable

Because of money laundering regulations, solicitors can only accept payments into bank accounts if they are from a UK bank or building society. If they are received from any other source then the solicitor is under an obligation to report the matter to the National Crime Agency (NCA).

Repaying a mortgage

If there is a mortgage on the property in question, this must be redeemed (paid off) on completion of the sale. Even if the mortgage is 'portable' then it is still has to be paid off. A redemption statement has to be obtained from the lender, detailing the amount outstanding from that lender against that property. You should take into account any redemption penalties.

The redemption statement is usually obtained at the beginning of the conveyance and then again at exchange of contracts.

Negative equity

If the amount to repay your mortgage is higher than the sale price, contracts cannot be exchanged until any shortfall has been made up. In virtually all cases, the mortgage is repaid in full on the day of completion by electronic transfer.

Now read the key points from chapter six.

****

KEY POINTS FROM CHAPTER SIX

- As with many other transactions, a sale of land is affected through a contract. The Law of Property Act, (Miscellaneous Provisions) 1988 provides that contracts dealing with the sale of land after 26th September 1989, must be in writing.If the phrase "subject to contract" is used then the intention of both parties to the contract is that neither are contractually bound until a formal contract has been agreed, signed and exchanged by the parties.

- Neither party is legally bound until there has been an exchange of contracts.

- Contracts are in two parts. The Particulars of Sale and the Conditions of Sale. The particulars give a physical description of the land and interest. There are two types of conditions, special and general. The latter is governed by the National Protocol for Domestic Leasehold and Freehold Property.

****

Chapter 7

Post-Completion

Completion of a land transaction will usually happen in the office of the vendor's solicitor. If there is an outstanding mortgage on the property and the mortgagee will not release the deeds until after payment has been made then completion will take place in the mortgagee's solicitors premises.

Completion will entail settling any outstanding payments between the vendor and purchaser. Also any legal work will be completed and deeds, if appropriate, will be handed over. On every transfer of sale of a freehold, lease or under-lease of seven years or more, the purchaser must complete a form giving particulars to HMRC. The form is to register the property for stamp duty and is known as "Stamps 1 (A) 451" or the "Particulars Delivered" form.

If the land is registered or being registered for the first time after completion, then if there is no Stamp duty land tax (SDLT) payable the particulars must be sent to the Land Registry together with an application for registration. In every other case, the deed and the particulars delivered form must be sent to HMRC within thirty days of completion. For example conveyancing fees other than Stamp duty refer to appendix 1.

Stamp duty land tax

You must pay Stamp Duty Land Tax (SDLT) if you buy a property or land over a certain price in England and Northern Ireland. The tax is different if the property or land is in:

- Scotland - pay Land and Buildings Transaction Tax
- Wales - pay Land Transaction Tax if the sale was completed on or after 1 April 2018

The current SDLT threshold is £125,000 for residential properties and £150,000 for non-residential land and properties. There are different rules if you're buying your first home. You get a discount (relief) that means you pay less or no tax if:

- you complete your purchase on or after 22 November 2017
- the purchase price is £500,000 or less
- you, and anyone else you're buying with, are first-time buyers

You pay the tax when you:

- buy a freehold property
- buy a new or existing leasehold
- buy a property through a shared ownership scheme
- are transferred land or property in exchange for payment, for example you take on a mortgage or buy a share in a house

How much you pay

How much you pay depends on whether the land or property is residential and whether you're a first-time buyer or non-residential or mixed-use. You may be able to reduce the amount of tax you pay by claiming relief, such as if you're a first-time buyer or purchasing more than one property ('multiple dwellings').

The value you pay SDLT on (the 'consideration')

The total value you pay SDLT on (sometimes called the 'consideration') is usually the price you pay for the property or land. Sometimes it might include another type of payment like:

- goods
- works or services
- release from a debt
- transfer of a debt, including the value of any outstanding mortgage

How and when to pay

You must send an SDLT return to HMRC and pay the tax within 14 days of completion. If you have a solicitor, agent or conveyancer, they'll usually file your return and pay the tax on your behalf on the day of completion and add the amount to their fees. They'll also claim any relief you're eligible for, such as if you're a first-time buyer. If they do not do this for you, you can file a return and pay the tax yourself.

Residential property rates

You usually pay Stamp Duty Land Tax (SDLT) on increasing portions of the property price above £125,000 when you buy residential property, for example a house or flat. There are different rules if you're buying your first home and the purchase price is £500,000 or less. You must still send an SDLT return for transactions under £125,000 unless they're exempt.

Rates on your first home

You can claim a discount (relief) so you do not pay any tax up to £300,000 and 5% on the portion from £300,001 to £500,000. You're eligible if:

- you, and anyone else you're buying with, are first-time buyers
- you complete your purchase on or after 22 November 2017

If the price is over £500,000, you follow the rules for people who've bought a home before.

Rates if you've bought a home before-Freehold sales and transfers

You can also use this table to work out the SDLT for the purchase price of a lease (the 'lease premium').

Property or lease premium or transfer value	SDLT rate
Up to £125,000	Zero
The next £125,000 (the portion from £125,001 to £250,000)	2%
The next £675,000 (the portion from £250,001 to £925,000)	5%
The next £575,000 (the portion from £925,001 to £1.5 million)	10%
The remaining amount (the portion above £1.5 million)	12%

Example If you buy a house for £275,000, the SDLT you owe is calculated as follows:

- 0% on the first £125,000 = £0
- 2% on the next £125,000 = £2,500
- 5% on the final £25,000 = £1,250
- Total SDLT = £3,750

New leasehold sales and transfers

When you buy a new residential leasehold property you pay SDLT on the purchase price of the lease (the 'lease premium') using the rates above. If the total rent over the life of the lease (known as the 'net present value') is more than £125,000, you also pay SDLT of 1% on the portion over £125,000 - unless you buy an existing ('assigned') lease.

Higher rates for additional properties

You'll usually have to pay 3% on top of the normal SDLT rates if buying a new residential property means you'll own more than one.

If you're replacing your main residence

You will not pay the extra 3% SDLT if the property you're buying is replacing your main residence and that has already been sold. If there's a delay selling your main residence and it has not been sold on the day you complete your new purchase:

- you'll have to pay higher rates because you own 2 properties
- you may be able to get a refund if you sell your previous main home within 36 months

There are special rules if you own property with someone else or already own a property outside England, Wales and Northern Ireland.

Special rates

There are different SDLT rules and rate calculations for:

- corporate bodies
- people buying 6 or more residential properties.
- shared ownership properties
- multiple purchases or transfers between the same buyer and seller ('linked purchases')
- purchases that mean you own more than one property
- companies and trusts buying residential property

Shared ownership property

You may have to pay Stamp Duty Land Tax (SDLT) when you buy a property through a shared ownership scheme run by an approved public body. This includes:

- local housing authorities
- housing associations
- housing action trusts
- the Northern Ireland Housing Executive
- the Commission for the New Towns
- development corporations

You can choose to either:

- make a one-off payment based on the market value of the property ('market value election')

- pay SDLT in stages

Market value election

Submit a return and pay SDLT at the residential rate. Use the total market value of the property to calculate how much to pay - even if you're only buying a share. You do not pay any more SDLT after this, even if you buy a bigger share in the property later on.

Example

You buy a 50% share of a property with a market value of £140,000. You have to pay SDLT of £300 (0% on £125,000 and 2% on £15,000). HM Revenue and Customs (HMRC) has guidance on SDLT if you do not have the right to the freehold.

Paying in stages

You make your first SDLT payment on the price you pay for the lease (the 'lease premium') if it's above the SDLT threshold. If the lease premium is below the threshold, you do not pay SDLT at this point - but you still have to submit a return. You may have to pay extra SDLT if the total rent over the life the lease (known as the 'net present value') is more than £125,000. You pay SDLT of 1% on the amount over £125,000 - add this to any SDLT you're paying on the lease premium.

SDLT if you buy more shares

If you buy any more shares in the property, you do not have to pay any more SDLT or send a return to HMRC until you own more than an 80% share.

Once your share of the property goes over 80% you must send a return and pay SDLT on:

- the transaction that took you over 80%
- any transactions after that

Calculating your SDLT

To work out the SDLT if you buy more shares that take you over 80%:

1. Work out the SDLT due on the total you've paid for the property to date (including any amounts you did not pay tax on). For example, if you've paid £160,000 in total so far, the total SDLT due is £700.

2. Divide the amount you're paying for this share by the total amount you've paid for the property to date. For example, if you're paying £40,000 for this share, divide £40,000 by £160,000 = 0.25.

3. Multiply the two figures, for example SDLT of £700 multiplied by 0.25 = £175. This is the amount you need to pay in SDLT for this share.

Additional tax if payments are linked

You may have to pay extra SDLT on previous shares if they become 'linked' to later shares. Shares only become linked once you own over 80% of the property.

Reliefs and exemptions

You may be eligible for Stamp Duty Land Tax (SDLT) reliefs if you're buying your first home and in certain other situations. These reliefs can reduce the amount of tax you pay. You must complete an SDLT return to claim relief, even if no tax is due. HM Revenue and Customs (HMRC) has guidance on SDLT reliefs for:

- first-time buyers
- multiple dwellings
- building companies buying an individual's home
- employers buying an employee's house
- local authorities making compulsory purchases
- property developers providing amenities to communities
- companies transferring property to another company
- charities
- right to buy properties
- registered social landlords

Exemptions

You do not have to pay SDLT or file a return if:

- no money or other payment changes hands for a land or property transfer
- property is left to you in a will
- property is transferred because of divorce or dissolution of a civil partnership
- you buy a freehold property for less than £40,000
- you buy a new or assigned lease of 7 years or more, as long as the premium is less than £40,000 and the annual rent is less than £1,000
- you buy a new or assigned lease of less than 7 years, as long as the amount you pay is less than the residential or non-residential SDLT threshold

- you use alternative property financial arrangements, for example to comply with Sharia law

****

Chapter 8

Conveyancing in Scotland

This chapter describes the general house buying process in Scotland, in addition to the steps in conveying a property. The main costs for buyers are:

- The interest on a mortgage (over a 25-year period, the interest on a typical repayment mortgage will be more than half the sum borrowed)
- Land and Buildings Transaction tax
- Mortgage arrangement fees
- Optional surveys
- Solicitor's fee
- Land registration fee

Land and Buildings Transaction tax

Home buyers must pay LBTT to the government as below (2019).

Tax Band	Normal rate	Additional dwelling
Less than £145,000	0%	4%**
£145,000 to £250,000	2%	6%
£250,000 to £325,000	5%	9%
£325,000 to £750,000	10%	14%
Rest over £750,000	12%	16%

* Percentage figures show LBTT and ADS rates combined. ADS is calculated in addition to LBTT and is applied at 4% to the total purchase price above £40k.
** An additional dwelling purchased for less than £40k will attract 0% tax. For purchases from £40k to £145k the rate will be 4% on the full purchase price.

Home Reports and Surveys

In the past, buyers had to arrange and pay for their own survey for each house they were interested in. These could cost several hundred pounds each. This has changed and the onus is now on the seller. Now, if you are selling a house in Scotland you must have a 'home report' prepared by a surveyor before marketing the property. Potential buyers no longer have to arrange or pay for surveys (although they may choose to have a separate survey done) and only one survey per property is needed. The home report is a survey similar to a normal survey but with other useful information included. Legally a home report must include the following items

A Single Survey

This contains the surveyor's assessment of the condition of the property, a valuation and an accessibility audit for people with particular needs.

An Energy Report

This contains the surveyor's assessment of the energy efficiency of the home and its environmental impact (including an Energy Performance Certificate). It also recommends ways to improve the energy efficiency of the property.

A Property Questionnaire

This gives other details about the property including council tax band, parking facilities, factoring arrangements, relevant local authority notices and alterations made to the home.

The home report is crucial in deciding whether to buy a particular house. It highlights any problems that need repaired and generally assesses the structural integrity and quality of the building inside and out.

The surveyor decides on a value for the property by taking into account the results of their inspection and current activity in the local property market. This value should be used as a guide or starting point for both the seller and buyer when agreeing a price. Valuation is not an exact science and the actual price a house might fetch always depends, to some extent, on how much a particular buyer is willing to pay to secure it.

The surveyor completing the report has a legal duty towards both the seller and the buyer to write an accurate report and can be held liable for losses arising as a result of errors. Potential buyers may decide to have their own survey carried out in addition to the home report, possibly because they want a more detailed assessment, or if their mortgage lender requires it. This should be done before making an offer.

Buyers can make an offer 'subject to survey' but sellers may be reluctant to accept an offer on that basis. The buyer's solicitor can advise them on the price and other matters that might affect their decision to buy the property, including local market conditions and trends and the prices which comparable local houses have fetched.

Noting Interest

If you are interested in a property but not at the stage of making an offer, you can instruct your solicitor to note your interest with the seller. This lets the seller know that you might make an offer so they can tell you if they set a 'closing date' (see below).

Closing Date

If a number of people show interest in a property, the seller may set a date which all offers need to be made by. They can then accept the highest offer. This is not the same as an auction, because bidders will have no knowledge of the other bids.

Making an Offer

Although most houses will be advertised as 'offers over', they may also be marketed as 'fixed price' or 'offers around'. In all cases, buyers and sellers can negotiate the actual price. Examples of issues that might affect the price a seller will accept are:

- How quickly they need to sell or move
- If the buyer pays cash
- If a survey reveals a lower value than the seller expected
- If the house has been on the market for a long time

In practice, the seller needs to be guided by the valuation in the home report. The actual price paid can be higher than the valuation if, for example:

- The buyer is extremely keen to buy the house
- There are a number of potential buyers competing to buy the house
- The buyer is in a hurry to move
- A separate survey gives a higher valuation

The buyer will need to bear all these factors in mind when instructing their solicitor to make an offer.

Missives

An offer to buy can be accepted relatively informally, even verbally. It is not binding at this point. Usually, the buyer's solicitor then sends the offer in writing to the seller's solicitor, who responds with a 'qualified acceptance' (a detailed document which basically says they accept the offer but only if certain conditions are met). These conditions are normally quite lengthy and may be designed to work in the seller's favour.

After consulting their client about the terms of the qualified acceptance, the buyer's solicitor then edits the document to make it more favourable to the buyer, and sends the edited version back to the seller's solicitor. This can continue back and forth until the seller agrees the terms and the final version is signed. The completed documents are called 'missives' and, once signed, they are a binding legal contract between the buyer and seller. The buyer must pay for and become the owner of the house, and do everything else agreed in the missives. The seller must allow ownership of the house to transfer to the buyer and allow them to move into it on the agreed date, and do everything else stated in the missives. Should either party withdraw or break the terms of the contract in some significant way, the other party can sue them for any losses incurred.

Examination of Title

The buyer's solicitor needs to check that the seller has a good title to the property (i.e. that they really own it and no-one else has any rights that could prevent a sale, such as a spouse with occupancy rights) and that the boundaries match those in the description given by the seller.

To check the title for most Scottish properties, a solicitor will examine the records held by the Registers of Scotland. A property's Land Certificate shows who the owner is and also includes details of any debts secured against it, along with details of title conditions (see below) and a plan of the property.

The current system of land registration is that the owner of a property is simply whoever the Land Certificate says is it is. People often refer to the Land Certificate as the 'deeds'.

Title Conditions

Ownership of property comes with conditions called burdens and servitudes which affect the owner's freedom to use the property as they wish. Common are servitudes granting a neighbour access along a shared drive or lane to get to their property, or burdens restricting the use of a property (for example, by prohibiting its use as a guest house). The buyer's solicitor should inform their client about all the title conditions before missives are concluded.

Title conditions can be very old and complex, and may not be in use anymore. For example, they may feature a time limit which has expired, or the issue they were intended to control is no longer relevant. If an owner breaks the terms of a title condition, other people who have some kind of right under it (neighbours) can seek to enforce it through the court. They may choose not to, or they may not even know about the title condition. They may be unsuccessful at court if they have not suffered any financial loss. This is a complex area of property law, and rights can even change over time depending on whether those who have them actually use them.

Standard Securities (Mortgages)

Standard Security is the correct Scottish legal term for a mortgage. It does not technically refer to the loan received from the lender, but is instead the name for the security that the owner grants to secure the debt. Any of the owner's debt can be secured against the property and, if he or she doesn't repay the debt, their creditor can ask a court to give them ownership of the property so they can sell it to recover as much of the debt as possible. As part of the purchase process, the buyer's solicitor needs to ensure that the buyer either has funds of their own to pay for the house, or has a mortgage loan agreed before missives are concluded. The solicitor will deal directly with the buyer's chosen lender to have the mortgage fully agreed and funds ready to transfer in time for settlement (see below).

Planning Permission

The buyer's solicitor must also check that the house and any alterations or extensions have been completed with the

91

appropriate planning permission. Sometimes it is necessary to get the local authority planning department to agree that they will not take action on works that have been carried out without permission.

Land Registration

The buyer's solicitor will also prepare the documents for the Registers of Scotland to have the buyer entered as the new owner of the property and the seller's Standard Security removed from the title. The buyer's Standard Security, if they have one, also needs to be added to the title.

Disposition

It is the job of the buyer's solicitor to prepare the disposition, the legal document that transfers ownership of the house from seller to buyer.

Settlement

- Settlement is the final step in the buying (and selling) process. It is the point at which money changes hands and the ownership of the house is legally transferred from the seller to the buyer. You need a Scottish solicitor to carry out the legal process of buying property in Scotland (conveyancing).
- The contract is binding once an offer is accepted in writing (when missives are completed) – there is no 'subject to contract' in Scotland

- Houses are usually sold on an 'offers over' basis in Scotland and the actual price is usually higher than the price advertised
- While in England the Home Information Pack is currently suspended, the Scottish equivalent (the Home Report) is in force and must be obtained by sellers before they can market a property

Help to Buy scheme

Scotland has a separate Help to Buy scheme from the one in England. It is available to all buyers of new build homes up to a maximum price of £400,000 and can contribute up to 20% of the cost of a home. The buyer needs to pay a 5% deposit and be able to borrow at least a further 75% of the cost of the home under a repayment mortgage.

The remainder is paid by the Scottish Government, which will have a separate Standard Security over the property. The buyer has full ownership of the property.

The money supplied by the Government gives them what is known as an 'equity stake'.

The buyer can then buy the Scottish Government's equity stake in instalments, or in full at a later date. There is, however, no requirement to buy the equity stake before the home is sold again. When it is sold, the Scottish Government is repaid from the proceeds of the sale.

To apply to the Help to Buy scheme you need to find a participating developer, and then speak to an independent financial advisor who can put you in touch with an agent who administers the scheme. An application is made to the agent, who decides whether you are eligible. If you are eligible, you will receive an 'authority to proceed' from the agent and you can then move forward with the mortgage application. The purchase process will need to be dealt with by a solicitor.

Now read the key points from Chapter 8 Overleaf.

****

KEY POINTS FROM CHAPTER 8

- You need a solicitor in order to buy a house in Scotland

- Once an offer has been accepted a binding contract follows

- The Home Report is a legal requirement in Scotland

- The buyer has to pay LBBT for houses costing more than £145,000

- Scotland has its own Help to Buy scheme that can contribute up to 20% of the cost of a new home

**

Conclusion and summary of the conveyancing process

This book is intended to be a guide to the processes of conveyancing in England and Wales and should be used in conjunction with a solicitor.

The book is very much about the procedures involved in buying and selling property. However, unless a conveyance is likely to be straightforward then you are advised to employ a solicitor or licensed conveyancer to carry out the work. Prices for such work are quite often very competitive and if there is a problem along the way then at least you have redress after the event. See appendix 1 for a breakdown of typical conveyancing costs.

In recognition of the fact that your head may be reeling after reading and digesting the factual information contained within this book, below is a simple step-by-step summary of the conveyancing process relating to the sale of a property.

Summary of conveyancing process

Step-by-step guide to the process
Before you get an offer

1. Decide who will do your conveyancing
  - Solicitors or licensed conveyancers can carry out conveyancing work.
  - It is possible to do it yourself but this is not recommended.

- Choose a 'no move, no fee' conveyancer – not one that charges by the hour.
- Avoid large conveyancing factories and conveyancing services recommended by online, hybrid or corporate estate agencies.
- Typically, conveyancing fees on a standard sale should cost (in total) approx. £600-£1,000.

2. Sign & return the conveyancing firm's Letter of Engagement

- To formally instruct a conveyancer or solicitor, you will receive a Letter of Engagement plus T&C's confirming the instruction and including details of their charges, including any which are payable in advance of the sale.
- You do not commit to using a conveyancing service until this letter has been signed and returned.

3. Provide proof of ID

- Your conveyancer will need to see copies of a photo driving licence or passport plus proof of your address, such as a mortgage statement or utility bill.

4. Complete and return the standard property information forms

- Your conveyancer will send you several forms including the Property Information Form (TA6) and the Fittings and Contents form (TA10).
- The sooner you complete these forms, the better to avoid unnecessary hold ups later down the line.

- You must be completely honest on these forms, or you could jeopardise the sale, or face being sued for compensation.
- If you are not sure about whether you want to leave the cooker or curtains, talk to your conveyancer, but normally they would say 'leave blank' or 'for negotiation' or even 'TBC'.
- You can confirm what to leave when you actually have an offer on the table.
- If your property is leasehold, you will also be given the Leasehold Information Form (TA7) and need to provide a copy of your lease.
- You or your legal representative will also need to obtain the Management Information Pack from the freeholder or managing agent. This can take several weeks to arrive so it's a good idea to request it as early as possible.

5. Send certificates, permission and guarantees
- Send your conveyancer copies of documents mentioned in any of the 'TA' property forms you fill in, such as guarantees and warranties for any work and building regulations sign-off for building work.
- Your conveyancer will send you a list of what is required.

6. Speak to your mortgage lender
- If you have a mortgage on your property, inform your lender or broker that you plan to sell and find out how much of the loan is outstanding and whether there is an early redemption penalty to pay.

- Your outstanding mortgage balance will be paid off on completion of the sale, unless you plan (and can) take the current mortgage with you to the next property – also known as porting.

From offer accepted to exchange

7. Have your solicitor send the draft contract to the buyer

- Once you have received and accepted an offer on your property, your solicitor or conveyancer will use all the information you provided, including the Property Information Form (TA6) and the Fixtures and Fittings form (TA10).
- This, together with any other information and the price accepted, will be used to draw up a draft contract to send to the buyer for approval.
- The draft contract will include information on:
-

1. Fixtures and fittings included in the sale price.
2. Price of any other fixtures and fittings available separately.
3. Covenants, warranties, guarantees, building control certificates and planning permission.
4. It may also include a provisional date of completion (usually two weeks after exchange, but this is not fixed).

8. Provide access for the buyer's survey

- The buyer will book a valuer and/or a surveyor to examine your home.

- This may flag up issues, which they wish to discuss or investigate further.

9. Renegotiate with the buyer
- If the survey flags up expensive work that is required – such as a damp proof course or roof repairs – the buyer may want to renegotiate the price to reflect this.
- Or they may ask you to carry out the repairs before they will exchange.

10. Help your conveyance answer enquiries
- As well as issues which arise from the survey, the buyer's solicitor or conveyancer may come back to you with further questions relating to the property searches – such as planning, drainage and environmental issues such as flooding – and the buyer may have their own questions, which aren't already answered in the Property Information Form.

11. Finalise contract & agree completion dates
- When the buyer and their legal representative are happy with the information your solicitor or conveyancer has provided, they will be sent the contract to read and sign.
- A completion date will be agreed to suit both parties.
- Up until contracts are exchanged, either party may pull out without penalty. Between exchange and completion your buyer can still pull out but you can sue them and may be able to keep the deposit.

From exchange to completion

12. Exchange contracts & receive deposit

The formal exchange of contracts usually takes place via a recorded telephone call between the two legal representatives working for the buyer and vendor.

- This can only take place when everybody in the chain is ready to proceed,
- Once contracts have been exchanged, your legal company will receive the agreed buyer's deposit.
- Be aware that the contract is now legally binding and you may not accept any further offers as, if you pull out now, the buyer may sue you for their legal costs.
- Similarly, if the buyer pulls out now, you may get to keep the deposit and sue them for your legal costs.

13. Get organised for your move

- Once you have exchanged, you now have until the completion date to organise removals, pack up your belongings and inform everybody of your move.
- This period is usually two weeks, although you can request a shorter or longer period if required and if everybody in the chain will agree.
- It is a good idea to go around your property before you complete to check the contents against the fixtures and fittings form. If you take something you shouldn't or leave things behind you should have taken, this can complicate and add stress to the day.

Completion day

14. Confirm your solicitor is 'in funds'

- Ideally, your solicitor or conveyancer will have received the balance payment for the property from your buyer's conveyancer the day before completion.
- On completion day, your conveyancer will:
1. Transfer the legal documents proving ownership to the buyer's conveyancer.
2. Organise the redemption of your mortgage and draw down any other monies.
3. Confirm the completion has taken place.
4. Pay any estate agent fees and conveyancer's fees out of the proceeds.
5. Send a completion statement including all the monies and ask you to pay any outstanding amounts owed.

15. Vacate the property

- Once completion has taken place, the property no longer belongs to you, so you must make sure you have vacated by this point and handed over the keys to your estate agent, leaving any spare sets inside the property.
- Typically, you should be out of your existing home by 1pm.
- This means in reality, most of your belongings need to be packed up the day before, unless you only have a small flat or few belongings.

****

A few simple words of advice

When buying property make sure that all debts are paid by the vendor before completing. This is especially pertinent to leasehold property that is quite often subject to a service charge. If the vendor does not settle debts then the purchaser will find his or her taking on the debt. Read contracts/leases very carefully indeed. Make sure that you know what it is that you are buying and that you are fully aware. Buying and selling property is a complex task-be very cautious and always scrutinise all documents very carefully. Make sure that what you buy is in sound condition and represents a good investment. It is the biggest investment that you will probably make.

****

Glossary

A

Acting for both parties-There are limited circumstances when solicitors can act for both parties

Amount outstanding on the mortgage-Also known as the redemption figure

Apportionment of the purchase price-This may be used to save stamp duty land tax. Fixtures and fittings known as chattels do not attract stamp duty and this is why the distinction between those and land is important.

Attorneys-A deed may be signed by an attorney but evidence of his power of attorney must be produced as this will be required by the land registry.

Auctions-The auction contract is usually prepared in advance The purchaser has the right to undertake all his searches en enquiries and survey before the auction. Once the auction has been concluded usually a ten percent deposit is taken and the sale takes place 28 days later. It would be necessary for anyone entering into an auction to have their finance in place before the hammer falls.

B

Boundaries-Even with a registered title the boundaries shown on the filed plan are general boundaries and are not definitive. The rule is generally what has been there for the last 12 years is the boundary. This may have to be supported by statutory declarations.

Bridging Finance-This might be for a deposit which is paid on the sale of the property. It is rare for English banks to extend finance for a property that is open ended. It is usually extended once contracts are exchange and there is a fixed completion.

Building Regulation Consent-This may be required even if there are not developments that require planning permission. It relates to health and safety matters and the type of materials used on completion of building works for which consent it required a final certificate must be obtained from the local authority. This is evidence that the building regulations have been complied with.

C

Capital Gains Tax-The main exemption which affects residential conveyancing is the principal private dwelling house exemption The seller must have occupied the dwelling house as his only or main residence throughout the period of ownership. There is a sliding scale for absences and exemptions of short periods of absence

Capacity-The seller might be sole owner, joint owner, personal representative mortgagee, charity, company bankrupt or otherwise incapacitated.

Classes of Title-There are different classes of title the best being absolute title but there is also possessory title qualified title and good leasehold title

Contaminated Land-Any contamination could have serious effects in that it may be impossible to sell or obtain a mortgage on a property.

Commonhold

A system of freehold tenure of a unit within a multi-occupancy building, but with shared responsibility for common services.

Completion-The day on which the transaction is finalised, the money changes hands and the parties vacate and take possession of the land.

Co-Ownership-This is where more than one person owns the land such as tenant in common or joint tenant.

Conveyancing-The process of transferring the ownership of freehold and leasehold land

Compulsory Registration-This has arisen since 1990 and applies to the whole of England and Wales. The categories of events triggering a registration have changed but it is still not compulsory to register land without one of these triggers. However, voluntary registration could take place.

Conservation Area-Any non-listed building in a conservation area must not be demolished without consent.

Contract Races-This is where more than one contract has been issued. Solicitors are obliged to let both parties know the terms of the race, that is what needs to be done to secure the property. It must be confirmed in writing. A standard contract race would specificy that the first person to be in a position to exchange contracts unconditionally wins the race. This is usually signified by the purchasers solicitors producing a signed contract and deposit together with authority to proceed.

Covenants-This is a promise made in a deed and binding any subsequent owner of the land. They may include such matter as maintaining the fences and only using the land for the erection of one property.

D

Deeds-Apart from unregistered land most deeds have now dematerialised as they are registered at the land registry.

Evidence of ownership is shown by official copies of the registered entries. This is an official dated document showing the current state of the title.

Deposit-Although not a legal requirement it is customary and it's a form of security and part-payment towards the purchase price.

Draft contract-The name attached to the contract before it is agreed by the parties and prior to exchange of contracts. Once the contract is approved it can be signed by the parties and forms the basis of the transactions. They must be in the same format so Identical contracts are exchanged.

E

Easements-This is a right over land of another such as a right of way or of light.

Engrossment-Merely means a properly typed up version of a document. The draft is amended then the engrossment is the fair copy

Escrow-A document such as contract mortgage transfer is delivered and will not become effective until some future date. It is therefore held in escrow the condition being that the event takes place such as completion or exchange of contract. Gets rid of the need for all the parties to a transaction being in the same room at the same time.

Exchange of contracts-When the parties agree to bind themselves legally to buy and sell the land

Execution-Means the signing of a document in a certain way for a deed to be valid. It must contain the words this deed signed by the necessary parties in the presence of a witness and be delivered.

F

Filed plan-In conveyancing a plan is a map showing the land referred to edged in red. It is the official designation of the land for land registry purposes.

Fixture and fittings-Now a formal part of the process in that purchasers solicitor will expect to see a completed fixtures and fittings form. It may be acceptable to apportion part of the price for fixtures and fittings and this is sometimes undertaken when the price falls on one of the bands for change in stamp duty. The list must be legitimate and HMRC have the right to query this and levy any tax not paid.

Fixtures and fittings distinction-This is between objects not attached to the land, which are fittings and those attached which are fixtures. The current fixtures and fitting list covers most eventualities but care should be taken if an offer is deemed to include items at the property. They should be specifically mentioned in the property fixtures form.

Full Survey-As the name suggests this is a full survey of the property and should contain a detailed breakdown of every aspect of the property.

H

Home Buyers Valuation and Survey Report-This is a compromise between a full structural survey and valuation.

I

Insurance-The risk on the property passes when contracts are exchanged, even though the purchaser has not got possession. The property is usually also insured by the seller up until the date of completion. They both have an insurable risk.

Indemnity Covenants- Any owner of land will remain liable for the covenants and passes these on by way of an indemnity covenant by any incoming purchaser.

Investigating Title-Once the seller has produced the contract package the purchasers solicitors investigate title. This is to ensure that the seller is the owner of the property which is the subject of the contract. Also it must not reveal any defects other than those that can be rectified prior to exchange of contracts. There may, for instance, be consent required from a third party such as the necessity to register the transfer of a lease and become the member of a management company.

J

Joint tenants-This is most common between husband and wife. Both own equal shares in the property and if either were to die the other inherits by way of survivorship. They cannot leave their share by will to anyone else.

L

Listed Building-Where a building might be of outstanding historic or architectural important the secretary of state may list it. Any alterations to the property will require both planning permission and listed building consent.

M

Mortgage-Is where the owner of land borrows money on the security of the land. Also known as a legal charge. The lender has certain statutory powers the most important being that they can sell the property in the event of the loan not being paid.

Mortgage Fraud-Normally some proof of identity is required but this has been overtaken by the money laundering rules whereby it is accepted practice that clients should produce to their solicitors all the usual forms of ID to include utility bills, driving licence, passport etc

Mortgages Repayments-The main types of repayment are pension, endowment and interest only. They do not affect the conveyancing transaction but some may have slightly different procedures between the conveyancers and the lender such as notices or deposit of insurance policies.

O

Occupiers Rights-The most important is the spouse of the seller. They have a statutory right to occupy the matrimonial home. Usually an enquiry is made as to there being any other occupiers of the matrimonial home. They are then asked to sign the contract to confirm they will give vacant possession completion.

Office Copy Entries-Usually refers to the registered title but can relate to any official copy issued by the land or other registries. They are acceptable as the originals.

Overriding Interests-These are matters affecting the land which are not on the register although this is being resolved under the current land registry rules. The most important being rights of way not mentioned on the deeds, local land charges and squatters rights.

P

Planning -Use of the property

It should be checked that the property has permission for its current use. Any purchaser should be aware that any change of

110

use from its current use may require planning permission. For example a residential property may not be used for the fixing and selling of cars without a change of use. Any breach will be enforced by the local planning authority.

Planning Breach-This could be rectified by retrospective permission or again by indemnity insurance.

Purchase Deed-Now the transfer or TR1 this is the document that is signed by the seller transferring the land from the seller to the purchaser. It is signed prior to completion and once the formalities have been finalised such as the passing of the money it will be forwarded to the purchasers solicitors. This document will need to be stamped and registered at the land registry.

Possessory Title-The registry may grant a possessory title in the event of lack of paper title and eventually it can be upgraded to an absolute title. Land can be acquired through adverse possession but it is still subject to all covenants and easements etc existing at the date of registration.

Post Contract Stage

Between exchange of contracts and completion essential things such as finance is resolved as are final searches and all documents signed in readiness for completion.

R

Radon-If the property is in an area affected by radon gas a specific search should be undertaken which will reveal whether a survey has been undertaken and remedial measures have been taken.

Registered land-A state run system that proves the ownership of land by having a title registered at HM land registry.

S

Searches-There are series of searches designed to elicit information about the property and the vendor

Special Conditions-Any special condition will be used to vary the standard conditions of sale contained in the contract

Subject to Contract-This is of historical interest now as it is not possible to exchange contracts inadvertently or entering into irrevocably buying land without a proper contract. Some organisations still insist on using it as it gives them comfort. It is not now necessary in view of the Law Of Property (Miscellaneous) Provisions Act 1989.

Survey-There are many kinds of survey from the mere valuation by a lender to a full structural survey. Any purchaser should be aware that the law says 'caveat emptor' that is let the buyer beware. Apart from a deliberate misstatement the seller is not liable for the current state of the property. A common practice is for purchasers to be advised to have a survey of the property and not to rely solely on the building society valuation.

T

Title-Either the registered or unregistered proof of the seller's ownership of the land

Title Number-Every piece of registered land has a unique title number and must be used in all official documents searches etc.

Tenants in Common-Is where two or more people own land jointly in separate shares. Either owner can pass their share by will to anyone they wish.

Tenure-The legal term for how the land is being held being either freehold or leasehold.

U

Unregistered Land-The seller has to prove title by a series of documents such as conveyances, mortgages etc.

Undertakings-These are promises by a solicitor to undertake certain acts, the most common being that the sellers solicitor will discharge the existing mortgage. Failure to comply with the undertaking is a professional offence so therefore they will not be entered into lightly and can be relied upon. They should always be confirmed in writing and their terms made certain.

Upgrading Title-Either on application or on the initiative of the registrar a title may be upgraded such as possessory to absolute and the same for qualified and good leasehold title.

V

Valuation-Can either be an estate agents valuation which is a financial matter for the purchasers and sellers. A lenders valuation is the figure that is used to calculate how much the lender is prepared to lend. This is based on a valuers report prepared for the lender once the buyer has requested a loan. Lenders will normally exclude liability for any defects in the property. They are not undertaking that the property is fit for its purpose just because they are prepared to lend on it.

Value Added Tax – VAT-Is payable on solicitors costs but not to the purchase price of second hand properties. There is no VAT payable on stamp duty or land registry fees in a domestic transaction.

W

Witnesses-Must be a responsible adult who is usually independent of the parties.

Appendix 1

SAMPLE STANDARD LETTERS USED IN CONVEYANCING

SALE OF PROPERTY
First Letter to Purchaser's Solicitors
29 May, 20

Address

Dear Sirs

Re   Property:
     Your Client:
     Our Client:

We understand that you act on behalf of in Connection with their proposed purchase of the above from our Clients .

We would be obliged if you could confirm that if your clients have a property to sell as a purchaser has been found and if your client should Require finance this has been approved at least in principle.

Subject to the above being confirmed we will arrange for a draft

Yours faithfully

Letter to Building Society / Bank requesting Title Deeds

29 May, 20

Address

Dear Sirs

Re   Property:
      Account Number:
      Borrower;

We act for the above named clients in connection with the sale of the above property and we shall be obliged if you would please send us the Title Deeds relating to this property.

We undertake to hold them to your order pending redemption of the mortgage.

At the same time please let us know the amount owing under this mortgage.

Yours faithfully

Authority to Bank to Obtain Title Deeds

29 May,20

Address

Dear Sirs

We hereby give you authority to release the Title Deeds for property listed below to………………of…………

Address of Property:
…………………………………………..

Address of Lender:
……………………………………………

Account Number:
……………………………………………….

Signature   ……………………………………………..

Letter Issuing Contract etc to Purchaser's Solicitors

29 May, 20

Address

Dear Sirs

Re   Property:
        Your Client;
        Our Client:

Thank you for your letter of . We take this opportunity of Enclosing:

Draft Contract in duplicate

Official Copy of Register Entries plus File Plan

Fixtures and Contents List

Seller's Property Information Form

Copy Transfer dated

Yours faithfully

Letter Sending Approved TR1 and Replies to Requisitions on Title

29 May,20

Address

Dear Sirs

Re   Property:
        Your Client:
        Our Client:

Thank you for your letter of ....we take this opportunity of enclosing the following:

TR1 approved as amended

Requisition on Title and our replies thereto

Yours faithfully

Letter to Purchaser's Solicitor on Exchange of Contracts

29 May, 20

Fax   &

Post

Fax

Number:

Address

Dear Sirs

Re   Property:
        Your Client:
        Our Client:

Further to our telephone conversation at 2:15 p.m. between…….
And …………..Contracts were exchanged and the date fixed for
Completion is ………………

The sale price £……….and you will be holding the £……….deposit
strictly to our order pending completion.

We enclose our client's part of the Contract to complete
exchange of contracts.

Yours faithfully

Letter to Bank / Building Society Requesting Redemption Figure

29 May, 20

Building Society

Address

Dear Sirs

Re: Borrower:

Property:

Account No:

Would you please let us have the redemption figure on the above mortgage account as at date……..

Yours faithfully

Appendix 2.
A Guide to Conveyancing fees

What are Conveyancing Fees?

Conveyancing fees are made up of the legal fee you will pay to your conveyancer for their service and the conveyancing disbursements that your conveyancer will pay on your behalf to third party services. The legal fee will be paid to your conveyancer for you using their service. Additionally, you'll have to pay disbursement fees for the transactions your conveyancer will do on your behalf. Most of the costs will come from the buyer's side of the transaction, but here are the main disbursement fees to consider:

- Environmental Searches
- Local Authority Searches
- Land Registry Searches
- Drainage Search
- Bank Transfer Fee
- Transferring Ownership
- Land Registry Title Deed Copies
- Stamp Duty Land Tax
- Telegraphic Transfer Fee

How Much are Conveyancing Fees?

The average conveyancing costs for buying a house is around £3,723, which includes £1,000 in conveyancing fees and £2,588 in disbursements. The disbursements are made up of £290 in search fees; £135 in Land Registry fees; £40 in transfer fees; £2 bankruptcy search, £6 land registry title deed search; and £2,115 in Stamp Duty.

The average conveyancing costs for selling a house is around £1,080, which includes £1,040 in conveyancing fees and a £40 transfer fee. These are estimates based on an average house price of £230,776 (December 2018 UK House Price Index).

Please note that this is just a guideline for an average cost and conveyancing fees will vary depending on the value of your home and the conveyancer that you choose to go with. It will cost more to purchase a leasehold property. You should use a moving house checklist to make sure you are fully prepared for all the costs of moving home.

Conveyancing Fees for Buying a House
Your conveyancer will charge a basic legal fee for the buying process, not including disbursement costs. An indication of legal costs are shown in the table below, followed by the additional disbursements. Conveyancing costs will be relative to your house price and the amount of work the solicitor has to do. Conveyancing fees will usually be fixed, and should be fully explained and costed.

It should be noted there is no one price for conveyancing fees and the price you pay will vary depending on the conveyancer, how much the house is worth, and the location of property.

*

Solicitors Fees for Buying a House (VAT included)
Property value   Avg Freehld cost
Avg leasehld cost

Property value	Avg Freehld cost	Avg leasehld cost
Up to £100,000	£860	£1,030
£100,001 to £200,000	£930	£1,110
£200,001 to £300,000	£1,040	£1,230
£300,001 to £400,000	£1,120	£1,310
£400,001 to £500,000	£1,200	£1,390
£500,001 to £600,000	£1,410	£1,560
£600,001 to £700,000	£1,440	£1,630
£700,001 to £800,000	£1,670	£1,850
£800,001 to £900,000	£1,810	£2,010
£900,001 to £1,000,000	£1,900	£2,100

Disbursement Costs when Buying a House

These are the extra costs paid by your solicitor to third parties on your behalf, called disbursements. Many are fixed price such as title deed searches, and others are relative to your house price such as Stamp Duty. The below are examples of average fees as at 2019. Some of the costs, such as the land registry, are fixed.

- Conveyancing Searches - £290
- Land Registry Title Deeds - £6

Your conveyancer has to prove that the seller is the legal owner of the house through obtaining official copies of the title deeds with the Land Registry.

Land Registry Transfer of Ownership - £135

Your conveyancer has to register you as the new owner of the property you are buying by transferring ownership with the Land Registry. This is relative to your house price, and will cost between £20 to £455 online, and between £40 and £910 by post. The transfer of ownership for a £230,000 house will cost £135.

Telegraphic Transfer Fee - £40

A telegraphic transfer will be a fee charged by the bank to transfer the money to your solicitor used for buying the house. This can cost between £25 to £35, but we found the average fee was around £40 when including VAT.

Stamp Duty Land Tax - £2,115

Stamp Duty will vary depending on the value of the property you're buying. The average homebuyer (£230,000) will spend around £2,115 on Stamp Duty. Cost will be different if paying the Wales Land Transaction Tax. If you're a first-time buyer buying a property under £300,000, then you are exempt from paying stamp duty.

Leasehold Disbursements

There are a few extra costs you can expect when purchasing a leasehold property. Conveyancers will increase legal fees when dealing with a leasehold property, simply because there's a large amount of extra work involved. The sample of conveyancers we looked at added an average of £230 in legal costs for leasehold compared to freehold properties.

On top of this, there are a range of extra disbursements faced by leaseholders. The cost of these disbursements do vary, and are usually set out in your lease.

Leasehold Cost	Disbursement
Landlord Sales Pack	£280
Notice of Transfer fee	£190
Notice of Charge fee	£140
Deed of Covenant	£280
Certificate of Compliance	£250

Conveyancing Fees for Selling a House

There's not as many conveyancing fees for selling as there are for buying a house. Below is an average conveyancing fee for selling a house, followed by other disbursements that come with selling a house.

It should be noted there is no one price for selling conveyancing fees and the price you pay will vary depending on the conveyancer, how much your house is worth, and the location of property.

Solicitor Fees for Selling a House (VAT included) (overleaf).

Property value	Avg Fhld Cost	Avg Lshold cost
Up to £100,000	£820	£990
£100,001 to £200,000	£880	£1,050
£200,001 to £300,000	£1,000	£1,170
£300,001 to £400,000	£1,090	£1,260
£400,001 to £500,000	£1,160	£1,340
£500,001 to £600,000	£1,330	£1,490
£600,001 to £700,000	£1,390	£1,550
£700,001 to £800,000	£1,600	£1,770
£800,001 to £900,000	£1,730	£1,880
£900,001 to £1,000,000	£1,840	£2,000

Disbursement Costs when Selling a House

Land Registry Title Deeds - £6
Getting land registry copies to the buyer's conveyancer will prove that you are the legal owner of the house you're selling.

Telegraphic Transfer Fee - £40
A telegraphic transfer fee is a cost when your conveyancer needs to transfer money, whether it's to pay off your mortgage or paying the final sale funds to your account.

When Do I Pay Conveyancing Fees?
If you're buying a property, you will have to pay upfront for the conveyancing searches that your conveyancer will order as the

council will require the money straight away. Additionally, you will have to pay fees to your conveyancer throughout the process and upon completion. Land Registry fees will have to be paid after completion.

If you're selling your house, there's a possibility you'll have to pay a small upfront cost. The rest will be paid throughout the conveyancing process and on completion day. Although each conveyancer is different, you may be required to pay their legal fee upfront or at the end of the process. Always make sure you ask for a breakdown of the quote and find out about any hidden or additional fees that could crop up to avoid a surprise bill.

What is Fixed Fee Conveyancing?
Fixed fee conveyancing means that you'll have pre-agreed a price for the job and it shouldn't change throughout the process as the conveyancer is offering a fixed fee. Make sure that it's clear what their fixed fee is offering and if it covers the disbursements and not just the basic conveyancing fee. By using a conveyancer who offers a fixed fee, you'll be able to budget and save money by knowing exactly how much it'll be. It's also important to see if the conveyancer is offering a 'no sale no fee' service, as this means if the sale was to fall through, you won't be charged the legal fees.

Fixed fee conveyancing is becoming increasingly popular now and it's rare that conveyancers will charge an hourly rate. Using a fixed fee service will work out cheaper as if any delays or issues were to crop up slowing down the process, you will still be charged per hour.

Additional Conveyancing Costs

There are a few circumstances that may incur extra costs. Conveyancing is usually a fixed fee, meaning you pay a set price for a set service. However there are a few common scenarios which will make the conveyancing process more complex, meaning extra work for your conveyancer and extra costs for you.

If the quote seems too cheap, then this likely won't cover the whole process of conveyancing costs. More often than not, the quote will just show the conveyancer's basic fee and won't include the cost of disbursements and additional hidden costs.

It's essential to read the small print and ask the conveyancer for the full itemised list of costs involved. Your quote breakdown should feature a full list of the disbursement services and how much they are. Ask if there are any additional or hidden costs that could be specific to your property, such as:

Leasehold Property - If you're selling a leasehold property, your conveyancer will charge more as this transaction is typically more time consuming. This usually costs an extra £100 – £200 plus VAT.

Private Draining Searches - If your conveyancer has to order searches on private draining, this will cost an additional £75-£150 plus VAT.

Solar Panel Documents - If you have solar panels at your new house, or are going to have some fitted, your conveyancer can charge between £100-£150 plus VAT to deal with the appropriate documents.

5 Days Between Exchange and Completion - Your conveyancer will charge between £100 - £200 plus VAT if you complete 5 days after exchanging contracts.

Common Extra Costs

These extra costs should be clearly outlined, though in some circumstances can come as a surprise if the upfront legal costs seem low.

Additional Services

	Cost
Help to Buy ISA	£60
Help to Buy Equity Loan	£300
Right to Buy	£230
Shared Ownership	£310
New Build	£290
Transfer of Equity	£530
Stamp Duty Return	£110

****

Appendix 3

Sample forms to be used in Residential Conveyancing

(overleaf)

Form 1. TA6 Property information form (14 pages)

Form 2. TA7 Leasehold Information Form (6 Pages)

Form 3. TA10 Fittings and Contents Form (7 pages)

Form 4. TR1. Transfer of whole (3 pages)

Property Information Form

Address of the property

Full names of the seller

Seller's conveyancer

Name of firm

Address

Email

Reference

This form is completed by the seller to supply detailed information and documents which may be relied upon for the conveyancing process. It is important that sellers and buyers read the notes below.

Definitions "Seller" means all sellers together if the property is owned by more than one person

"Buyer" means all buyers together if the property is being bought by more than one person.

"Property" includes all the buildings and land within the boundaries

Instructions to the Seller • Answers should be prepared by the person or persons who are named as owner on the deeds or Land Registry title or by the owner's legal representative(s) if selling under a power of attorney or grant of representation. If there is more than one seller, you should prepare the answers together or, if only one seller prepares the form, the other(s) should check the answers given and all sellers should sign the form.

- If you do not know the answer to any question, you must say so. If you are unsure of the meaning of any questions or answers, please ask your conveyancer. Completing this form is not mandatory, but omissions or delay in providing some information may delay the sale.

- If you later become aware of any information which would alter any replies you have given, you must inform your conveyancer immediately. This is as important as giving the right answers in the first place. Do not change any arrangements concerning the property with anyone (such as a tenant or a neighbour) without first consulting your conveyancer.

- It is very important that your answers are accurate. If you give incorrect or incomplete information to the buyer (on this form or otherwise in writing or in conversation, whether through your estate agent or conveyancer or directly to the buyer), the buyer may make a claim for compensation from you or refuse to complete the purchase.

- You should answer the questions based upon information known to you (or, in the case of legal representatives, you or the owner). You are not expected to have expert knowledge of legal or technical matters, or matters that occurred prior to your ownership of the property.

- Please give your conveyancer any letters, agreements or other papers which help answer the questions. If you are aware of any which you are not supplying with the answers, tell your conveyancer. If you do not have any documentation you may need to obtain copies at your own expense. Also pass to your conveyancer any notices you have received concerning the property and any which arrive at any time before completion of the sale.

Instructions to the buyer

- If the seller gives you, separately from this form, any information concerning the property (in writing or in conversation, whether through an estate agent or solicitor or directly to you) on which you wish to rely when buying the property, you should tell your conveyancer.

- You are entitled to rely on the replies given to enquiries but in relation to the physical condition of the property, the replies should not be treated as a substitute for undertaking your own survey or making your own independent enquiries, which you are recommended to do.

- The seller is only obliged to give answers based on their own information. They may not have knowledge of legal or technical matters. You should not expect the seller to have knowledge of, or give information about, matters prior to their ownership of the property.

1 Boundaries

1.1 Looking towards the property from the road, who owns or accepts responsibility to maintain or repair the boundary features:

(a) On the left?

☐ Seller ☐ Neighbour
☐ Shared ☐ Not known

(b) On the right?

☐ Seller ☐ Neighbour
☐ Shared ☐ Not known

(c) At the rear?

☐ Seller ☐ Neighbour
☐ Shared ☐ Not known

(d) At the front?

☐ Seller ☐ Neighbour
☐ Shared ☐ Not known

1.2 If the boundaries are irregular please indicate ownership by written description or by reference to a plan:

1.3 Is the seller aware of any boundary feature having been moved in the last 20 years? If Yes, please give details:

☐ Yes ☐ No

1.4 During the seller's ownership, has any land previously forming part of the property been sold or any adjacent property purchased? If Yes, please give details:

☐ Yes ☐ No

1.5 Does any part of the property or any building on the property overhang, or project under, the boundary of the neighbouring property or road? If Yes, please give details:

☐ Yes ☐ No

1.6 Has any notice been received under the Party Wall Act 1996 in respect of any shared/party boundaries? If Yes, please supply a copy, and give details of any works carried out or agreed:

☐ Yes ☐ No
☐ Enclosed ☐ To follow

2   Disputes and complaints

2.1   Have there been any disputes or complaints regarding this property or a property nearby?   If Yes, please give details: ☐ Yes   ☐ No

2.2   Is the seller aware of anything which might lead to a dispute about the property or a property nearby?   If Yes, please give details: ☐ Yes   ☐ No

3.   Notices and proposals

3.1   Have any notices or correspondence been received or sent (e.g. from or to a neighbour, council or government department), or any negotiations or discussions taken place, which affect the property or a property nearby?   If Yes, please give details: ☐ Yes   ☐ No

3.2   Is the seller aware of any proposals to develop property or land nearby, or of any proposals to make alterations to buildings nearby?   If Yes, please give details: ☐ Yes   ☐ No

4.   Alterations, planning and building control

Note to seller: Please provide copies of all relevant approvals and supporting paperwork referred to in section 4 of this form, such as listed building consents, planning permissions, Building Regulations consents and completion certificates. If you have had works carried out you should produce the documentation authorising this. Copies may be obtained from the relevant local authority website. Competent Persons Certificates may be obtained from the contractor or the scheme provider (eg FENSA or Gas Safe Register). *For further information about Competent Persons Certificates go to: www.gov.uk.*

Note to buyer: If any alterations or improvements have been made since the property was last valued for council tax, the sale of the property may trigger a revaluation. This may mean that following completion of the sale, the property will be put into a higher council tax band. *For further information about council tax valuation go to: www.voa.gov.uk.*

4.1 Have any of the following changes been made to the whole or any part of the property (including the garden)?

(a) Building works (eg extension, loft or garage conversion, removal of internal walls). If Yes, please give details including dates of all work undertaken

☐ Yes   ☐ No

(b) Change of use (eg from an office to a residence)

☐ Yes   ☐ No

[ ] Year

(c) Installation of replacement windows, roof windows, roof lights, glazed doors since 1 April 2002

☐ Yes   ☐ No

[ ] Year(s)

(d) Addition of a conservatory

☐ Yes   ☐ No

[ ] Year

4.2 If Yes to any of the questions in 4.1 and if the work was undertaken during the seller's ownership of the property:

(a) please supply copies of the planning permissions, Building Regulations approvals and Completion Certificates, OR:

(b) if none were required, please explain why these were not required – e.g. permitted development rights applied or the work was exempt from Building Regulations:

For further information about permitted development go to: www.planningportal.gov.uk

4.3 Are any of the works disclosed in 4.1 above unfinished? If Yes, please give details

☐ Yes   ☐ No

4.4 Is the seller aware of any breach of planning permission conditions or Building Regulations consent conditions, unfinished work or work that does not have all necessary consents? If Yes, please give details:

☐ Yes   ☐ No

4.5 Are there any planning or building control issues to resolve? If Yes, please give details:

☐ Yes   ☐ No

4.6 Have solar panels been installed? If Yes: ☐ Yes   ☐ No

    (a) in what year were the solar panels installed? `[_____]` Year

    (b) are the solar panels owned outright? ☐ Yes   ☐ No

    c) has a long lease of the roof/air space been granted to a solar panel provider? If Yes, please supply copies of the relevant documents ☐ Yes   ☐ No ☐ Enclosed   ☐ To follow

4.7 Is the property or any part of it:

    (a) A listed building? ☐ Yes   ☐ No ☐ Not known

    (b) In a conservation area? ☐ Yes   ☐ No ☐ Not known

    If Yes, please supply copies of any relevant documents. ☐ Enclosed   ☐ To follow

4.8 Are any of the trees on the property subject to a Tree Preservation Order? ☐ Yes   ☐ No ☐ Not known

    If Yes:

    (a) Have the terms of the Order been complied with? ☐ Yes   ☐ No ☐ Not known

    (b) Please supply a copy of any relevant documents. ☐ Enclosed   ☐ To follow

5. Guarantees and warranties

Note to seller: Please supply all available guarantees, warranties and supporting paperwork before exchange of contracts.

Note to buyer: Some guarantees only operate to protect the person who had the work carried out or may not be valid if their terms have been breached. You may wish to contact the company to establish whether it is still trading and if so, whether the terms of the guarantee will apply to you.

5.1 Does the property benefit from any of the following guarantees or warranties? If Yes, please supply a copy.

    (a) New home warranty (eg NHBC or similar) ☐ Yes   ☐ No ☐ Enclosed   ☐ To follow

    (b) Damp proofing ☐ Yes   ☐ No ☐ Enclosed   ☐ To follow

    (c) Timber treatment ☐ Yes   ☐ No ☐ Enclosed   ☐ To follow

    (d) Windows, roof lights, roof windows or glazed doors ☐ Yes   ☐ No ☐ Enclosed   ☐ To follow

(e) Electrical work

☐ Yes   ☐ No
☐ Enclosed   ☐ To follow

(f) Roofing

☐ Yes   ☐ No
☐ Enclosed   ☐ To follow

(g) Central heating

☐ Yes   ☐ No
☐ Enclosed   ☐ To follow

(h) underpinning

☐ Yes   ☐ No
☐ Enclosed   ☐ To follow

(i) Other (please state)

☐ Enclosed   ☐ To follow

5.2 Have any claims been made under any of these guarantees or warranties? If Yes, please give details

☐ Yes   ☐ No

6 Insurance

6.1 Does the seller insure the property?

☐ Yes   ☐ No

6.2 Has any buildings insurance taken out by the seller ever been:

(a) Subject to an abnormal rise in premiums?

☐ Yes   ☐ No

(b) Subject to high excesses?

☐ Yes   ☐ No

(c) Subject to unusual conditions?

☐ Yes   ☐ No

(d) Refused?

☐ Yes   ☐ No

If Yes, please give details:

6.3 Has the seller made any buildings insurance claims? If Yes, please give details:

☐ Yes   ☐ No

Flooding

Note: Flooding may take a variety of forms: it may be seasonal or irregular or simply a one-off occurrence. The property does not need to be near a sea or river for flooding to occur. *For further information about flooding go to: www.defra.gov.uk.*

7.1   Has any part of the property (whether buildings or surrounding garden or land) ever been flooded? If Yes, please state when the flooding occurred and identify the parts that flooded:

☐ Yes   ☐ No *(go to 7.3)*

7.2   What type of flooding occurred?

(a)   Ground water   ☐ Yes   ☐ No

(b)   Sewer flooding   ☐ Yes   ☐ No

(c)   Surface water   ☐ Yes   ☐ No

(d)   Coastal flooding   ☐ Yes   ☐ No

(e)   River flooding   ☐ Yes   ☐ No

(f)   Other (please state):   ☐ Yes   ☐ No

7.3   Has a Flood Risk Report been prepared? If Yes, please supply a copy.

☐ Yes   ☐ No
☐ Enclosed   ☐ To follow

For further information about the types of flooding and Flood Risk Reports go to: www.environment-agency.gov.uk.

Radon

Note: Radon is a naturally occurring inert radioactive gas found in the ground. Some parts of England and Wales are more adversely affected by it than others. Remedial action is advised for properties with a test result above the "recommended action level". *For further information about Radon go to: www.hpa.org.uk.*

7.4   Has a Radon test been carried out on the property? If Yes:

☐ Yes   ☐ No

(a)   Please supply a copy of the report

☐ Enclosed   ☐ To follow

(b)   Was the test result below the "recommended action level"?

☐ Yes   ☐ No

7.5   Were any remedial measures undertaken on construction to reduce Radon gas levels in the property?

☐ Yes   ☐ No
☐ Not Known

Energy Efficiency

Note: An Energy Performance Certificate (EPC) is a document that gives information about a property's energy usage. *For further information about EPCs go to www.gov.uk.*

7.6   Please supply a copy of the EPC for the property

☐ Enclosed   ☐ To follow

☐ Already supplied

7.7   Have any installations in the property been financed under the Green Deal scheme? If Yes, please give details of all installations and supply a copy of your last electricity bill.

☐ Yes   ☐ No

☐ Enclosed   ☐ To follow

For further information about the Green Deal go to: www.gov.uk/decc.

Japanese knotweed

Note: Japanese knotweed is an invasive plan that can cause damage to property. It can take several years to eradicate.

7.8   Is the property affected by Japanese knotweed?

☐ Yes   ☐ No

☐ Not known

If Yes, please state whether there is a Japanese knotweed management plan in place and supply a copy

☐ Yes   ☐ No

☐ Not known

☐ Enclosed   ☐ To follow

8   Rights and informal arrangements

Note: Rights and arrangements may relate to access or shared use. They may also include leases of less than seven years, rights to mines and minerals, manorial rights, chancel repair and similar matters. If you are uncertain about whether a right or arrangement is covered by this question, please ask your conveyancer.

8.1   Does ownership of the property carry a responsibility to contribute towards the cost of any jointly used services, such as maintenance of a private road, a shared driveway, a boundary or drain? If Yes, please give details:

☐ Yes   ☐ No

8.2   Does the property benefit from any rights or arrangements over any neighbouring property? If Yes, please give details:

☐ Yes   ☐ No

8.3 Has anyone taken steps to prevent access to the property, or to complain about or demand payment for access to the property? If Yes, please give details:

☐ Yes   ☐ No

8.4 Does the seller know of any of the following rights or arrangements affecting the property:

(a) Rights of light ☐ Yes ☐ No

(b) Rights of support from adjoining properties ☐ Yes ☐ No

c) Customary rights (eg rights deriving from local traditions) ☐ Yes ☐ No

(d) Other people's rights to mines and minerals under the land ☐ Yes ☐ No

e) Chancel repair liability ☐ Yes ☐ No

(f) Other people's rights to take things from the land (such as timber, hay or fish) ☐ Yes ☐ No

If Yes, please give details:

8.5 Are there any other rights or arrangements affecting the property? If Yes, please give details:

☐ Yes   ☐ No

Services crossing the property or neighbouring property

8.6 Do any drains, pipes or wires serving the property cross any neighbour's property?

☐ Yes   ☐ No
☐ Not known

8.7 Do any drains, pipes or wires leading to any neighbour's property cross the property?

☐ Yes   ☐ No
☐ Not known

8.8 Is there any agreement or arrangement about drains, pipes or wires?

☐ Yes   ☐ No
☐ Not known

If Yes, please supply a copy or give details:

☐ Enclosed   ☐ To follow

9 Parking

9.1 What are the parking arrangements at the property?

9.2 Is the property in a controlled parking zone or within a local authority parking scheme?

☐ Yes ☐ No
☐ Not known

10 Other charges

Note: If the property is leasehold, details of lease expenses such as service charges and ground rent should be set out on the separate Leasehold Information Form. If the property is freehold, there may still be charges; for example, payments to a management company or for the use of a private drainage system.

10.1 Does the seller have to pay any charges relating to the property (excluding any payments such as council tax, utility charges etc). If Yes, please give details

☐ Yes ☐ No

11 Occupiers

11.1 Does the seller live at the property?

☐ Yes ☐ No

11.2 Does anyone else, aged 17 or over, live at the property?

☐ Yes ☐ No
Go to section 12

11.3 Please give the full names of any occupiers (other than the seller) aged 17 or over:

11.4 Are any of the people named in 11.3 tenants or lodgers?

☐ Yes ☐ No

11.5 Is the property being sold with vacant possession?

☐ Yes ☐ No

If Yes, have all the occupiers aged 17 or over:

(a) Agreed to leave prior to completion?

☐ Yes ☐ No

(b) Agreed to sign the sale contract? If No, please supply other evidence that the property will be vacant on completion.

☐ Yes ☐ No
☐ Enclosed ☐ To follow

12 Services

Note: If the seller does not have a certificate requested below this can be obtained from the relevant Competent Persons Scheme. *For further information about Competent Persons Schemes go to: www.gov.uk*

Electricity

12.1   Has the whole or any part of the electrical installation been tested by a qualified and registered electrician?

☐ Yes   ☐ No

If Yes, please state the year it was tested and provide a copy of the test certificate.

[   ] Year

☐ Enclosed   ☐ To follow

12.2   Has the property been rewired or had any electrical installation work carried out since 1 January 2005?

☐ Yes   ☐ No

☐ Not known

If Yes, please supply one of the following:

(a)   A copy of the signed BS7671 Electrical Safety Certificate

☐ Enclosed   ☐ To follow

(b)   The installer's Building Regulations Compliance Certificate

☐ Enclosed   ☐ To follow

c)   The Building Control Completion Certificate

☐ Enclosed   ☐ To follow

Central heating

12.3   Does the property have a central heating system? If Yes:

☐ Yes   ☐ No

(a)   What type of system is it (eg mains gas, liquid gas, oil, electricity, etc)?

[   ]

(b)   When was the heating system installed? If on or after 1 April 2005 please supply a copy of the "completion certificate" (eg CORGI or Gas Safe Register) or the "exceptional circumstances" form.

[   ] Date

☐ Not known

☐ Enclosed   ☐ To follow

c)   Is the heating system in good working order?

☐ Yes   ☐ No

(d)   In what year was the heating system last serviced/maintained? Please supply a copy of the inspection report.

[   ] Year   ☐ Not known

☐ Enclosed   ☐ To follow

☐ Not available

Drainage and sewerage

Note: *For further information about drainage and sewerage go to: www.environment-agency.gov.uk* .

12.4   Is the property connected to mains:

(a)   Foul water drainage?

☐ Yes   ☐ No

☐ Not known

(b)   Surface water drainage?

☐ Yes   ☐ No

☐ Not known

If Yes to both questions, go to section 13. If No, please answer the following questions:

12.5   Is sewerage for the property provided by:

(a)   A septic tank?

☐ Yes   ☐ No

(b)   A sewage treatment plant?

☐ Yes   ☐ No

(c)   Cesspool?

☐ Yes   ☐ No

12.6 Is the use of the septic tank, sewage treatment plant or cesspool shared with other properties? If Yes, how many properties share the system?

☐ Yes ☐ No

☐ Properties share

12.7 When was the system last emptied?

☐ Year

12.8 If the Property is served by a sewage treatment plant, when was the treatment plant last serviced?

☐ Year

12.9 When was the system installed?

☐ Year

Note: Some systems installed after 1 January 1991 require Buildings Regulations approval, environmental permits or registration. *For further information about permits and registration go to: www.environment-agency.gov.uk*

12.10 Is any part of the septic tank, sewage treatment plant (including any soakaway or outfall) or cesspool, or the access to it, outside the boundary of the property? If Yes, please supply a plan showing the location of the system and how access is obtained.

☐ Yes ☐ No

☐ Enclosed ☐ To follow

13 Connection to utilities and services

Please mark the Yes or No boxes to show which of the following utilities and services are connected to the property and give details of any providers.

Mains electricity ☐ Yes ☐ No	Mains gas ☐ Yes ☐ No
Providers' name	Provider's name
Location of meter	Location of meter

Mains water ☐ Yes ☐ No	Mains sewerage ☐ Yes ☐ No
Providers' name	Provider's name
Location of stopcock	
Location of meter, if any	

Telephone ☐ Yes ☐ No	Cable ☐ Yes ☐ No
Providers' name	Provider's name

14 Transaction information

14.1 Is this sale dependent on the seller completing the purchase of another property on the same day?

☐ Yes ☐ No

14.2   Does the seller have any special requirements about a moving date? If Yes, please give details:

☐ Yes   ☐ No

14.3   Does the sale price exceed the amount necessary to repay all mortgages and charges secured on the property?

☐ Yes   ☐ No

14.4   Will the seller ensure that:

(a)   All rubbish is removed from the property (including from the loft, garden, outbuildings, garages and sheds) and that the property will be left in a clean and tidy condition?

☐ Yes   ☐ No

(b)   If light fittings are removed, the fittings will be replaced with ceiling rose, flex, bulb holder and bulb?

☐ Yes   ☐ No

(c)   Reasonable care will be taken when removing any other fittings or contents

☐ Yes   ☐ No

(d)   Keys to all windows and doors and details of alarm codes will be left at the property or with the estate agent?

☐ Yes   ☐ No

Signed..   Dated.................................

Signed..   Dated.................................

All sellers should sign this form

Leasehold Information Form (2nd edition)   TA7

Address of the Property

Full names of the seller

Seller's Solicitor

Name of Solicitors firm

Address

Email

Reference Number

Definitions

- 'Seller' means all sellers together where the property is owned by more than one person

- 'Buyer' means all buyers together where the property is being bought by more than one person

- 'Property' means the leasehold property being sold

- 'Building' means the building containing the property

- 'Neighbour' means those occupying flats in the building

Instructions to the seller

The seller should provide all relevant documentation relating to the lease when they return this completed form to their solicitor. This may include documents given to the seller when they purchased the property, or documents subsequently given to the seller by those managing the property.

Instructions to the seller And the buyer

Please read the notes on *TA6 Property Information Form*

1 The property

1.1 What type of leasehold property does the seller own? ('Flat' includes maisonette and apartment).

☐ Flat

☐ Shared ownership

☐ Long leasehold house

1.2 Does the seller pay rent for the property? If Yes:

☐ Yes   ☐ No

(a) How much is the current yearly rent?

[＿＿＿＿＿] £

(b) How regularly is the rent paid (e.g. yearly)?

[＿＿＿＿＿] Payments

2 Relevant documents

2.1 Please supply a copy of:

(a) the lease and any supplemental deeds

☐ Enclosed   ☐ To follow

☐ Already supplied

(b) any regulations made by the landlord or by the tenants' management company additional to those in the lease

☐ Enclosed   ☐ To follow

☐ Not applicable

2.2 Please supply a copy of any correspondence from the landlord, the management company and the managing agent.

☐ Enclosed   ☐ To follow

2.3 Please supply a copy of any invoices or demands and any statements and receipts for the payment of:

(a) maintenance or service charges for the last three years

☐ Enclosed   ☐ To follow

☐ Not applicable

(b) ground rent for the last three years

☐ Enclosed   ☐ To follow

☐ Not applicable

2.4 Please supply a copy of the buildings insurance policy:

(a) arranged by the seller and a receipt for payment of the last premium, **or**

☐ Enclosed   ☐ To follow

(b) arranged by the landlord or management company and the schedule for the current year

☐ Enclosed   ☐ To follow

2.5 Have the tenants formed a management company to manage the building? If Yes, please supply a copy of:

☐ Yes   ☐ No

(a) the Memorandum and Articles of Association

☐ Enclosed   ☐ To follow

(b) the share or membership certificate

☐ Enclosed   ☐ To follow

(c) the company accounts for the past three years

☐ Enclosed   ☐ To follow

3 Management of the building

3.1 Does the landlord employ a managing agent to collect rent or manage the building?

☐ Yes ☐ No

3.2 Has any management company formed by the tenants been dissolved or struck off the register at Companies House?

☐ Yes ☐ No
☐ Not known

3.3 Do the tenants pass day-to-day responsibility for the management of the building to managing agents?

☐ Yes ☐ No

4 Contact details

4.1 Please supply contact details for the following, where appropriate. (The landlord may be, for example, a private individual, a housing association, or a management company owned by the residents. A managing agent may be employed by the landlord or by the tenants' management company to collect the rent and/or manage the building.)

	Landlord	Managing agent contracted by the landlord
Name		
Address		
Tel		
Email		

	Managing agent contracted by the tenants' management company
Name	
Address	
Tel	
Email	

5.1   Who is responsible for arranging the buildings insurance on the property?

☐ Seller

☐ Management company

☐ Landlord

5.2   In what year was the outside of the building last decorated?

☐ Year   ☐ Not known

5.3   In what year were any internal communal parts last decorated?

☐ Year   ☐ Not known

5.4   Does the seller contribute to the cost of maintaining the building?

☐ Yes   ☐ No

If No to question 5.4, please continue to section 6 'Notices' and do not answer questions 5.5–5.9 below.

5.5   Does the seller know of any expense (e.g. the cost of redecoration of outside or communal areas not usually incurred annually) likely to be shown in the service charge accounts within the next three years? If Yes, please give details:

☐ Yes   ☐ No

5.6   Does the seller know of any problems in the last three years regarding the level of service charges or with the management? If Yes, please give details:

☐ Yes   ☐ No

5.7   Has the seller challenged the service charge or any expense in the last three years? If Yes, please give details:

☐ Yes   ☐ No

5.8   Is the seller aware of any difficulties encountered in collecting the service charges from other flat owners? If Yes, please give details:

☐ Yes   ☐ No

5.9 Does the seller owe any service charges, rent, insurance premium or other financial contribution? If Yes, please give details:

☐ Yes ☐ No

---

6 Notices

Note: A notice may be in a printed form or in the form of a letter.

6.1 Has the seller received a notice that the landlord wants to sell the building? If Yes, please supply a copy.

☐ Yes ☐ No
☐ Enclosed ☐ To follow
☐ Lost

6.2 Has the seller received any other notice about the building, its use, its condition or its repair and maintenance? If Yes, please supply a copy.

☐ Yes ☐ No
☐ Enclosed ☐ To follow
☐ Lost

---

7 Consents

Note: A consent may be given in a formal document, a letter or orally.

7.1 Is the seller aware of any changes in the terms of the lease or of the landlord giving any consents under the lease? If Yes, please supply a copy or, if not in writing, please give details:

☐ Yes ☐ No
☐ Enclosed ☐ To follow
☐ Lost

---

8 Complaints

8.1 Has the seller received any complaint from the landlord, the management company or any neighbour about anything the seller has or has not done? If Yes, please give details:

☐ Yes ☐ No

8.2 Has the seller complained or had cause to complain to or about the landlord, the management company, or any neighbour? If Yes, please give details:

☐ Yes ☐ No

---

9 Alterations

9.1 Is the seller aware of any alterations having been made to the property since the lease was originally granted?

☐ Yes ☐ No

If No, please go to section 10 'Enfranchisement' and do not answer 9.2 and 9.3 below.

9.2 Please give details of these alterations:

9.3 Was the landlord's consent for the alterations obtained? If Yes, please supply a copy.

☐ Yes ☐ No
☐ Not known ☐ Not required
☐ Enclosed ☐ To follow

---

10 Enfranchisement

Note: 'Enfranchisement' is the right of a tenant to purchase the freehold from their landlord and the right of the tenant to extend the term of the lease.

10.1 Has the seller owned the property for at least two years?

☐ Yes ☐ No

10.2 Has the seller served on the landlord a formal notice stating the seller's wish to buy the freehold or be granted an extended lease? If Yes, please supply a copy.

☐ Yes ☐ No
☐ Enclosed ☐ To follow
☐ Lost

10.3 Is the seller aware of the service of any notice relating to the possible collective purchase of the freehold of the building or part of it by a group of tenants? If Yes, please supply a copy.

☐ Yes ☐ No
☐ Enclosed ☐ To follow
☐ Lost

10.4 Is the seller aware of any response to a notice disclosed in replies to 10.2 and 10.3 above? If Yes, please supply a copy.

☐ Yes ☐ No
☐ Enclosed ☐ To follow
☐ Lost

Signed: .... Dated: ....

Each seller should sign this form.

Fittings and Contents Form

Address of the property

Full names of the seller

Seller's conveyancer

Name of firm

Address

Email

Reference

This form is completed by the seller to supply detailed information and documents which may be relied upon for the conveyancing process. It is important that sellers and buyers read the notes below.

Definitions
"Seller" means all sellers together if the property is owned by more than one person

"Buyer" means all buyers together if the property is being bought by more than one person.

Instructions to the Seller
This form must be completed accurately by the seller, who should check through all answers before signing it. It may become part of the contract between the seller and the buyer.

The seller should indicate clearly what is included in the sale of the property by marking each box on this form

- With a tick
- A question mark if not decided or for discussion
- If the item is excluded, the seller may insert a price for the item. The buyer can then decide whether to accept the seller's offer to sell the item. The seller and buyer should inform their conveyancers of any arrangements made about items offered for sale in this way.

If an item is offered for sale, it is the seller's responsibility to negotiate the sale with the buyer directly, or through their estate agent (if applicable). If the conveyancer is instructed to act in the negotiation, the costs of so doing may not be included in the original quote and may be subject to additional charges.

If the seller removes any fixtures, fittings or contents, the seller should be reasonably careful to ensure that any damage caused is minimised.

Unless stated otherwise, the seller will be responsible for ensuring that all rubbish is removed from the property (including from the loft, garden, outbuildings, garages and sheds), and that the property is left in a reasonably clean and tidy condition.

The buyer should check the information given by the seller in this form carefully.

1   Basic fittings

	Included	Excluded	None	Price	Comments
Boiler/immersion heater					
Radiators/wall heaters					
Night-storage heaters					
Free-standing heaters					
Gas fires (with surround)					
Electric fires (with surround)					
Light Switches					
Roof insulation					
Window fittings					
Window shutters/grilles					
Internal door fittings					
External door fittings					
Doorbell/chime					
Electric sockets					
Burglar alarm					

Other basic fittings (please state which)					

2 | Television and telephone

	Included	Excluded	None	Price	Comments
Telephone receivers					
Television aerial					
Radio aerial					
Satellite dish					

3 | Kitchen

Note: for each, please indicate whether the item is fitted or freestanding and whether it is included or excluded.

	Fitted	Free-standing	Included	Excluded	None	Price	Comments
Hob							
Extractor hood							
Oven/grill							
Cooker							
Microwave							
Refrigerator/fridge-freezer							
Freezer							
Dishwasher							
Tumble-dryer							
Washing machine							

4 | Bathroom

	Included	Excluded	None	Price	Comments
Bath					
Shower fitting for bath					
Shower curtain					
Bathroom cabinet					
Taps					

Separate shower and fittings					
Towel rail					
Soap/toothbrush holders					
Toilet roll holders					
Bathroom mirror					

5 Carpets

	Included	Excluded	None	Price	Comments
Hall, stairs and landing					
Living room					
Dining room					
Kitchen					
Bedroom 1					
Bedroom 2					
Bedroom 3					
Other rooms (please specify)					

6 Curtains and curtain rails

	Included	Excluded	None	Price	Comments
Curtain rails/poles/pelmets					
Hall, stairs and landing					
Living room					
Dining room					
Kitchen					
Bedroom 1					
Bedroom 2					
Bedroom 3					
Other rooms (please specify)					

Curtains/blinds					
Hall, stairs and landing					
Living room					
Dining room					
Kitchen					
Bedroom 1					
Bedroom 2					
Bedroom 3					
Other rooms (please specify)					

7 Light fittings

	Included	Excluded	None	Price	Comments
Hall, stairs and landing					
Living room					
Dining room					
Kitchen					
Bedroom 1					
Bedroom 2					
Bedroom 3					
Other rooms (please specify)					

If the seller removes a light fitting, it is assumed that the seller will replace the fitting with a ceiling rose, a flex, bulb holder and bulb and that they will be left in a safe condition.

8 Fitted units

(For example: fitted cupboards, fitted shelves and fitted wardrobes)

	Included	Excluded	None	Price	Comments
Hall, stairs and landing					
Living room					
Dining room					
Kitchen					

Bedroom 1					
Bedroom 2					
Bedroom 3					
Other rooms (please specify)					

9 Outdoor area

	Included	Excluded	None	Price	Comments
Garden furniture					
Garden ornaments					
Trees, plants, shrubs					
Barbecue					
Dustbins					
Garden shed					
Greenhouse					
Outdoor heater					
Outside lights					
Water butt					
Clothes line					
Rotary line					
Other items					

10 Stock of fuel

	Included	Excluded	None	Price	Comments
Oil					
Wood					
Bottled gas					
LPG					

11 | Other items

	Included	Excluded	None	Price	Comments

Signed.. Dated...............................

Signed.. Dated...............................

All sellers should sign this form

If you need more room than is provided for in a panel, and your software allows, you can expand any panel in the form. Alternatively use continuation sheet CS and attach it to this form.

Leave blank if not yet registered.	1	Title number(s) of the property:
Insert address including postcode (if any) or other description of the property, for example 'land adjoining 2 Acacia Avenue'.	2	Property:
	3	Date:
Give full name(s).	4	Transferor:
Complete as appropriate where the transferor is a company.		**For UK incorporated companies/LLPs** Registered number of company or limited liability partnership including any prefix: **For overseas companies** (a) Territory of incorporation: (b) Registered number in England and Wales including any prefix:
Give full name(s).	5	Transferee for entry in the register:
Complete as appropriate where the transferee is a company. Also, for an overseas company, unless an arrangement with Land Registry exists, lodge either a certificate in Form 7 in Schedule 3 to the Land Registration Rules 2003 or a certified copy of the constitution in English or Welsh, or other evidence permitted by rule 183 of the Land Registration Rules 2003.		**For UK incorporated companies/LLPs** Registered number of company or limited liability partnership including any prefix: **For overseas companies** (a) Territory of incorporation: (b) Registered number in England and Wales including any prefix:
Each transferee may give up to three addresses for service, one of which must be a postal address whether or not in the UK (including the postcode, if any). The others can be any combination of a postal address, a UK DX box number or an electronic address.	6	Transferee's intended address(es) for service for entry in the register:
	7	The transferor transfers the property to the transferee

Place 'X' in the appropriate box. State the currency unit if other than sterling. If none of the boxes apply, insert an appropriate memorandum in panel 11.

8   Consideration

☐ The transferor has received from the transferee for the property the following sum (in words and figures):

☐ The transfer is not for money or anything that has a monetary value

☐ Insert other receipt as appropriate:

Place 'X' in any box that applies.

Add any modifications.

9   The transferor transfers with

☐ full title guarantee

☐ limited title guarantee

Where the transferee is more than one person, place 'X' in the appropriate box.

10   Declaration of trust. The transferee is more than one person and

☐ they are to hold the property on trust for themselves as joint tenants

☐ they are to hold the property on trust for themselves as tenants in common in equal shares

Complete as necessary.

☐ they are to hold the property on trust:

Insert here any required or permitted statement, certificate or application and any agreed covenants, declarations and so on.

11   Additional provisions

The transferor must execute this transfer as a deed using the space opposite. If there is more than one transferor, all must execute. Forms of execution are given in Schedule 9 to the Land Registration Rules 2003. If the transfer contains transferee's covenants or declarations or contains an application by the transferee (such as for a restriction), it must also be executed by the transferee.

12   Execution

Index

Abstract of title, 41

Bankruptcy, 5, 71
Business leases, 18

Chancel repair search, 32
Charge Certificate, 57
City of London Corporation, 27
Commonhold and Leasehold Reform Act 2002, 13, 17
Commons Registration Act (1965), 31
Companies Act 1989, 47
Company searches, 45
Compulsory registration, 53
Conditions of sale, 5, 68
Contract For sale, 63
Council of Licensed Conveyancers, 7
Covenants, 15, 106, 109

Dematerialisation, 57
Disposition, 6, 92

Encumbrances, 14
Energy Performance Certificate, 86
Energy Report, 5
Enquiries before contract, 25, 26
Examination of Title, 5, 90
Exchanging contracts, 4, 65

First Registration of title, 53
First Tier Tribunals, 16
Freehold transfer document, 10

Scotland, 85, 86, 90, 92, 93, 95
Searches, 3, 25, 31, 33, 112
Seller's property information forms, 26
Service charge, 10
Settlement, 6, 92
Special conditions, 68
Stamp duty land tax, 75
Standard Security, 91, 92, 93

Testatum, 4, 46
Testimonium, 4, 47
Title Conditions, 5, 90

Underlease, 66
Unregistered land, 11, 19, 41

Words of grant, 4, 46

****